BEYOND REACH

Also by William Hoffman

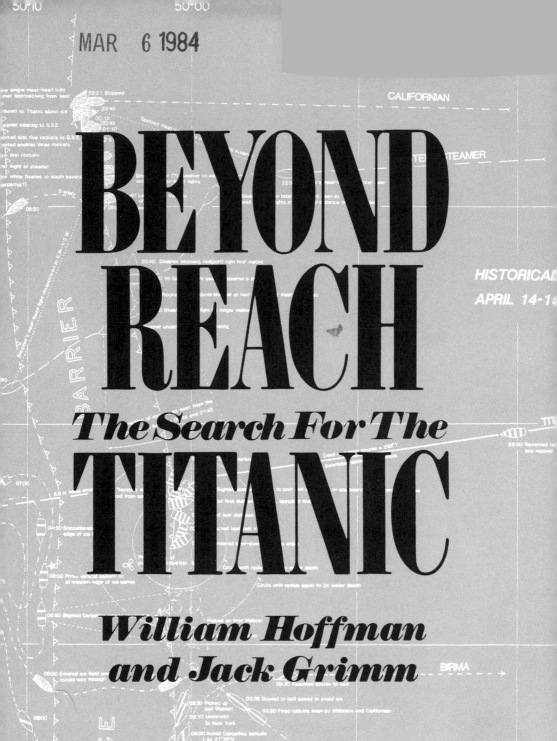

BEYOND REACH

The Search For The

TITANIC

William Hoffman
and Jack Grimm

BEAUFORT BOOKS, INC.

New York / Toronto

Library of Congress Cataloging in Publication Data

Hoffman, William, 1937–
   Beyond reach.

   1. Titanic (Steamship)   I. Title.
G530.T6H63   622'.19   82-4298
ISBN 0-8253-0105-X   AACR2

Published in the United States by Beaufort Books, Inc., New York.
Published simultaneously in Canada by General Publishing Co. Limited

Printed in the U.S.A.   First Edition
10 9 8 7 6 5 4 3 2 1
Design by Ellen LoGiudice

I want to thank William, Joe,
Terri, and John Hoffman,
Eric Protter, Judy, Ethan,
Lea, and Micah Lewis,
and B. J. Billing.

TO: All those on the *Gyre,*
and to their families, also.

CONTENTS

BEYOND
REACH

"*An iceberg, sir. I hard-a-starboarded and reversed the engines, and I was going to hard-a-port around it, but she was too close. I couldn't do any more.*"

—William M. Murdoch,
First Officer, R.M.S. *Titanic*,
April 14, 1912

THE FOUNDERING

To call him charismatic would be to exaggerate, but he did manage to be both well liked and respected.

Thomas Andrews went about his life positively, with his rich, throaty laugh, and telling stories with the best of the tale-tellers in the shipyard. He helped those he could, and disciplined those who required it. He was, in the words of one of his foremen, "One of nature's gentlemen."

He was an imperialist. He was a unionist, afraid that financial ruin would be wrought upon his native Ireland if home rule was imposed. He supported social reform, especially where labour was concerned. The men at the yard were not mere pals, he felt, and both men and masters needed fair and reasonable rules, not governmental controls.

Perhaps more than anything, Thomas Andrews believed in the Protestant work ethic. By choice, his own workday was long, and before his marriage even his spare hours were spent studying—

machine and freehand drawing, applied mechanics, the theory of naval architecture. His diligence was well-known at the shipyard of Messrs. Harland & Wolff, where he had risen from apprentice to Managing Director. His belief in work was at least in part the product of a profound confidence that his hours of labor were helping mankind progress to a higher or better state. But not to perfection, for Thomas Andrews, in his wife's words, had "of himself the humblest opinion of anyone I ever knew."

It was his confidence in progress and diligence that resulted in his being at his desk at 11:40 P.M. that night. In Stateroom A-36 he studied the charts, plans, and notes that covered his desk. More rolls of blueprints lay beside his bed a few feet away. With the trained eye of a man who had spent twenty-three years building ships, Andrews compared the paperwork with the real ship. As the designer who rendered an idea onto paper, Andrews was proud to be aboard what was at that moment the largest and greatest ship on the seas, a symbol of Britain's strength, a monument to industrial progress. He was aboard the Royal Mail Ship *Titanic* on her maiden voyage.

She was by no means perfect. He felt that there were too many screws in the stateroom hat hooks. There was considerable space wasted in the reading and writing room on the Promenade Deck (the ladies hadn't taken to it) so he planned to divide one section of the room into two additional staterooms. His instinct for color balance also told him that the wicker furniture on one side of the ship ought to be stained green, but they were such trivial concerns that occupied him as he wrote his nightly letter to his beloved wife waiting back in Belfast with their two-year-old daughter.

The day had passed without incident. Always up with the sun, Andrews had been inspecting the ship from early morning. The five years' hard work since the ship's conception was done. Complete as well were the final, rigorous checks and rechecks by both the Board of Trade, with its volume of regulations, and the meticulous Mr. Andrews. For Andrews the first two days after casting off from Southampton had been tense, though he knew well and trusted every inch of his newest ship.

Perhaps it was only that Sunday evening, April 14, after the ship had been at sea two full days, that he relaxed. The engines six decks beneath him drove the sharp prow of the *Titanic* smartly through the icy-cold waters of the North Atlantic at the equivalent of twenty-six miles per hour. His steward, Samuel Etches, had laid out his dress clothes for dinner, in the mannered and graceful way of the day, and had helped Andrews dress. Andrews had gone to the first-class dining room, and joined his friend Dr. W. F. O'Loughlin. As the venerable senior surgeon of the White Star Line, the old doctor was—like many of the crew members aboard the *Titanic*—rewarded for his long and distinguished service to the company by being asked to serve on the first crossing on the *Titanic*, the biggest, most luxurious, and most ballyhooed ship of the day.

Few people would have felt it appropriate to call Andrews by his Christian name, let alone by its diminutive. But to the amiable ship's surgeon Managing Director Thomas Andrews would always be "Tommy." Their dinner was, as was the rule on the White Star Line, well prepared and suitable for a class of people capable of paying thousands of dollars for a transatlantic passage. Andrews, having recovered from a slight indisposition no doubt caused by his nervousness over the new ship putting to sea, ate heartily. A stewardess said later, "He was in good spirits, and I thought he looked splendid."

In the smoking room after dinner, Andrews confided to a passenger. The perfectionist designer and builder was finally satisfied with his ship. "I believe her to be as nearly perfect as human brains can make her," he said.

*

No moon shone that night. The sea was strangely smooth, a mirror of the motionless sky above, where millions of stars offered an illusory illumination.

Numerous marconigrams had been received by the *Titanic*'s radio operators, warning of a sea cluttered with icebergs. Small bergs, called growlers, reach as little as three feet out of the water but weigh as much as one hundred tons. The larger chunks of ice sometimes reach three hundred feet out of the water and weigh a million-and-a-half tons, nine-tenths of it below the water.

Both large and small bergs are born generations before their launching on Greenland's icecap. The excruciatingly slow motion of the glacier, crunching southward at an imperceptible pace, moves ice off the shore and into the sea. The process of the ice breaking off, called calving, sends the chunks off on their own.

Many icebergs remain in their native coves for a year or two before drifting into currents that deliver them south. From the western shore of Greenland, they coast past eastern Canada and Newfoundland, irrevocably and silently floating into the busy North Atlantic shipping lanes. By mid-April the icebergs are at their peak in size and frequency.

Andrews had no knowledge that in the path of his ship a huge icefield awaited. A nearby ship was already surrounded by ice. The *Californian* had shut down its engines, to wait until morning to proceed. But the *Titanic* raced on, its engines powering the ship full speed ahead.

The berg that awaited was probably not a giant, and protruded some one hundred feet out of the water. On that clear night a light mist may have obscured it slightly. To further lessen its visibility, as Second Officer Lightoller later testified, one side of the iceberg—as is often so with the portion of the berg that calves away from the glacier—was black. On that moonless night the diligent officers on watch and the two lookouts high in the crow's nest saw nothing until suddenly, out of the blackness, something emerged.

At first, the lookout who spied the ice thought it was the size of two dining tables put together. It loomed larger and larger. He signaled to the bridge. The officer on watch responded quickly and ordered a hard turn to the port. The enormous ship, despite the efforts of the men, seemed not to obey, but to lumber on as if unafraid of the ever larger chunk of rock-hard ice straight ahead. At the last second, the prow began to swing. The iceberg, in an awesome silence, scraped the starboard side.

The impact was little more than a shudder and was felt little or not at all on the upper decks. In Andrew's cabin the impact was so slight it escaped his notice. He was attuned to his ship as a sculptor is to his creation, but the sheer size of it protected him from the realization his creation had been assaulted. He went on writing.

A knock on his door drew his attention. A sailor, in a polite but abrupt manner, summoned him to the bridge. "The captain wants . . ."

When he got there, Captain Edward J. Smith, another much honored veteran of the White Star Line, told Andrews what had happened. The two of them quickly descended into the bowels of the ship.

"The Queen of the Ocean," as the advertisements had hailed her, had been widely proclaimed to be unsinkable. The *Titanic* was divided from prow to stern into sixteen watertight compartments. Immediately after the collision, the doors between them had, with the flick of an electrical switch, slammed closed. With the doors closed throughout, the distinguished technical journal *Shipbuilder* had intoned in a special 1911 edition, the "vessel [is made] practically unsinkable."

The captain and Andrews went down the crew's stairway in order not to draw attention to their task. They walked past the Number 5 Boiler Room on the lowest deck. It was filling rapidly with water. They walked toward the bow to the mailroom on the lower deck, only one level above the ship's double bottom. Adjacent was the squash rackets court, a new and much admired innovation to the ship.

All told, six of the sixteen compartments were filling with sea water. As if that were not enough, Andrews suddenly realized because the transverse bulkheads that divided the ship into its separate "watertight" compartments only reached the deckheads, as soon as the gush of water reached that level, it would—like water in an overflowing bathtub—splash over the edge into the next compartment. All sixteen compartments—and thus, the entire, gracious, unsinkable *Titanic*, were doomed. She had been designed to float with any two compartments flooded (who could imagine any more than two?).

As the captain and Andrews clambered back up the eight levels to the bridge, the shipbuilder calculated. The flooding in the six forward compartments was evidence of a gash not less than 300 feet in length, 10 feet above the level of the keel. Although the pumps were hard at work, the water was flowing in far faster than it could be pumped out.

The two men walked quickly through the A-Deck foyer, which had filled with anxious passengers wondering why the engines had stopped. No one was able to read the looks on the faces of Captain Smith or Andrews.

The conclusion was inescapable, if almost unspeakable. The *Titanic* was on her way to the ocean floor, some thirteen thousand feet of salt water below. Andrews told the captain he estimated the ship had but ninety minutes left.

Captain Smith gave the order, and the bo'sun piped the dreaded words: "All hands up and get the lifeboats ready!"

Just after midnight on the morning of April 15, 1912, the first SOS signal ever transmitted went out on the airwaves. Radio communication was itself relatively new and still a series of dots and dashes. No message was simple, and many required repeating, or even replaying from one receiving ship or port to another.

"CQD MGY" went out first, the first three letters being the

usual international distress call, come quickly disaster, and *MGY* the call letters of the *Titanic*. It was so simple anyone could pick it up. Toward the end, as a last ditch effort, the SOS was sent. Besides, as one radio operator said to the other, "Send SOS; it's the new call, and it may be your last chance to send it."

As the word went out to ships within range that the *Titanic* was in trouble, the news also traveled around the ship. The most common reaction was disbelief: the unsinkable *Titanic* in danger of foundering? Preposterous.

Not only the passengers, who for the most part had not had much experience with the awesome strength of the sea and its disrespect for mere man-made ships, but also the crew, who should have known better, responded with incredulity. In one room of crew's quarters below decks, it took harsh words and the invocation of the respected Mr. Andrews's name to bring home the truth. "Turn out, you fellows," the boatswain called, " . . . you haven't half an hour to live. That is from Mr. Andrews."

Meanwhile, the water flooded in. Because the gash lanced compartments at the ship's prow, the water was filling those compartments first, and the ship no longer floated levelly, but listed to one side, and her bow sat lower in the water than her stern. The engines—stopped a moment after impact—were silent, but the boilers still maintained a full head of steam. It escaped into the frigid night air, its hissing a roar that was inhibiting the instructions of the crew as they loaded the lifeboats.

Andrews was below decks to help get the more than two thousand on board organized. He instructed one of the stewardesses on how to prepare the passengers. "Tell them to put on warm clothing, see that everyone has a life belt and get them all up to the Boat Deck."

He instructed another stewardess, "Open all the spare rooms. Take out all life belts and spare blankets and distribute them."

Andrews was, as always, carrying the trust of others, dealing with the problems of those who came to him. Even on what was to be the last night of his life—and he knew it, as he never donned a life belt, never attempted to climb into a lifeboat—he offered calm, reasoned encouragement. To the very same passenger in whom he had confided only hours earlier of the ship's near perfection, he said, "There is no cause for any excitement. All of you get what you can in the way of clothes and come on deck as soon as you can. She is torn to bits below, but she will not sink if her after bulkheads hold."

His role that night was to help as many people survive as possible. When he bumped into the same stewardess on A Deck whom he had instructed to open up the spare rooms, he spoke to her in the tone of a schoolmaster not so much cross at the students as disappointed that the lesson was not learned. "Did I not tell you to put on your life belt?"

"Yes," she replied slowly, "but I thought it mean to wear it."

"Never mind that," he told her. "Now, if you value your life, put on your coat and belt, then walk round the deck and let the passengers see you."

To a third stewardess he confided the truth. "It is very serious, but keep the bad news quiet for fear of panic."

No formal warning had been given, no formal announcement was broadcast for all to hear. It wasn't necessary. The crew manning the lifeboats swung each lifeboat out over the cold ocean, working the davits and ropes. They loaded each and lowered them. Again, it was Andrews, knowing the workings of the boats' tackle, who aided the crew—they had never had a drill with the lifeboats—in getting them safely lowered.

The first lifeboat to go had been lowered seventy feet. As others followed, the task grew easier. Sixty feet became fifty, then forty and less. The *Titanic*, moment by moment, was slipping inch-by-inch into the sea, as it poured into her holds. Her balance became ever more precarious, as her list grew more pronounced. It was becoming harder to walk across the deck.

As the water crept inexorably up the stairways toward the Boat

Deck on which the crowd stood watching the lifeboats fill, Andrews was heard to say, "Now, men, remember you are Englishmen. Women and children first."

Beginning at 12:45 A.M. signal rockets had been sent skyward. The fireworks were the most dramatic way of getting the attention of any ship within sight, and many who survived the sinking recall the sight of a ship, seemingly only a few miles away. For anyone on board the *Titanic* still holding a false hope the accident was minor, that it was just a drill, their hope was gone.

Eight rockets shot toward the heavens, according to most accounts. The last of them, some twenty minutes from the end, seemed to signal a similar flash, but of a human kind. For the first and only time in the entire two hours and forty minutes—between the delivery of the death blow by the berg and the foundering of the ship—people panicked.

Few lifeboats remained, and some passengers and crew were coming to the realization that there were not enough seats in the lifeboats for everyone on board. In fact, less than half of those on board would have fit into the boats, even if they had been dropped into the ocean full up. Some of the boats, designed for forty or more people, left with as few as twelve.

There was a crush of people near the davits that still held lifeboats. Some women and children seemed hesitant to clamber into the boats, though the ship's deck was at such a slant there could be no doubt as to the danger. Andrews, again on the scene, took charge.

His instructions were clear. "Ladies, you must get in at once. There is not a minute to lose. You cannot pick and choose your boat. Don't hesitate. Get in, get in!"

It was five minutes past two, and though no one could have gauged it precisely, the R.M.S. *Titanic* had but fifteen minutes more afloat. The forecastle head was already under water, yet the seven-piece band, under the direction of Wallace Henry Hartley, played on in the first-class lounge. Ironically, the music they played was upbeat, lilting ragtime.

Not more than two hundred feet aft, Thomas Andrews stood in the first-class smoking room, his arms crossed and resting on his chest. The last of the lifeboats were gone. He stood alone. According to the testimony of a steward who happened through during those moments, Andrews "just stood like one stunned."

He stared at a painting, "The Approach of the New World." One has to think he wasn't seeing it but was lost in reverie. Perhaps he was thinking of his last instruction to his secretary as the *Titanic* set sail from Southampton. "Remember now and keep Mrs. Andrews informed of any news of the vessel," he had said.

He knew now what news she would get of his and the *Titanic*'s fate. Andrews had probably realized within seconds of seeing the evidence of the great gash in the hull that the ship would go down. The American politician was right when, only days later at an inquiry in Washington, he said, "The awful force of the impact was well-known to the master [Captain E. J. Smith] and builder, Mr. Andrews, who from the first must have known the ship was doomed. . . . The builder, whose heart must have broken when he realized he had not prepared that ship to resist a blow so dangerous, seemed to have been quite willing to go down with the ship."

The room in which he stood was as richly appointed as any ever to be found on board a ship. No photographs remain, but among the elegant decorative touches were richly carved wainscotting; leaded glass windows portraying matters nautical and notable; a lush patterned rug; and serpentine, candelabralike wall fixtures for the electric lights. The solid, over-stuffed chairs and heavy mahogany card tables bespoke of an age of confidence, of a belief in statements made boldly and loudly, that things were as they ought to be.

As Andrews stood staring, seeing nothing, bemused at the imminent foundering of his ship, a steward, likewise stunned and more than a little awed at the sight of dynamic Mr. Andrews frozen in time, noticed Andrews's life belt resting on a table.

"Aren't you going to have a try for it, Mr. Andrews?"

When he received no answer, nor even an acknowledgment of his words, the steward left quickly, not at all conflicted about his desire to "have a try for it."

Andrews remained behind, still staring aft.

The band played on. All the boats were gone, yet more than fifteen hundred passengers remained aboard the doomed *Titanic*.

Where Andrews was, no one knows. Reports place him racing to the bridge to bid Captain Smith farewell, in the engine room working with the engineers to keep lights on and the pumps at work. Other witnesses claimed to have seen him just moments before the end, throwing deck chairs overboard to those already in the water. He may well have remained in the smoking room, impassive, lost in his tortured thoughts about what had gone wrong. It hardly matters.

He was a positive man, though not a man of hubris, so perhaps he simply accepted the inevitability of his fate, and spent his last moments recalling a happy childhood (before the age of ten he gained the nickname Admiral). Perhaps he thought of his bees (not only did he keep a number of hives, but, according to his biographer, Shan Bullock, his favorite book with which to relax was Maeterlinck's *Life of the Bee*).

Maybe his thoughts ran back just before the turn of the century, when he was Head of the Repair Department. He had engineered a pair of remarkable feats when he and his workers had actually lengthened a pair of ships, the *Scot* and the *Augusta Victoria*, by chopping the ships in two and inserting sections amidships. Perhaps for a fleeting moment he pondered the possibility of the *Titanic* in dry dock, the staunching of her wound receiving the attention of scores of men under the direction of Thomas Andrews, shipbuilder.

Wherever he was, he surely felt the bow of the great ship dip deep into the sea. The hundreds of passengers on deck ran aft, in a vain attempt to escape the sea. Her stern swung upward, and a wave surged up the deck, carrying many into the sub-freezing salt water. The music had stopped—the last strains were from the Episcopal hymn "Autumn," neither ragtime nor "Nearer My God to Thee," as legend has it. The lights still blazed, and from the lifeboats the submerged portions of ship had a gauzelike cast.

As the ship's tilt grew steeper, it tipped more quicky. Accounts vary, but all agree on the fearsome tumult that ensued. Few individual sounds were distinguishable, but as if to contribute to the chaos the lights failed as the ship tipped precipitously. Screams went unheard as everything on shipboard that wasn't bolted down fell toward the bow, drawn by the inexorable pull of gravity. First one, then another of the funnels fell over. The twenty-nine massive boilers tumbled free and crashed through the hull. As the stern swung out of the water, the three propellers cleaved the air, powerless and immobile.

The *Titanic* stood perfectly perpendicular to the North Atlantic for perhaps a minute, maybe two. It was poised for its monumental final dive. It looked to those passengers shivering in the lifeboats as if the ship were frozen in time.

Then, as if some greater force released its grip, the ship began to sink. Imperceptibly at first, then more quickly, the giant slid into the ocean. Its speed increasing, it disappeared, like a perfectly balanced knife.

In the light of day on April 15, only hours after the *Titanic* had plunged, headlong, to the ocean floor, the German ship *Prinz Adalbert* sighted an iceberg with what appeared to be a scraping of red paint at its base. At best it is idle speculation to wonder whether it was the very iceberg with which the great *Titanic* had collided, but it may have been the same one, its surface portion looking like some rock-hard mountain tor that had appeared, as if by magic, and ripped the great tear in the *Titanic*'s unsinkable hull.

Those who saw that red-stained berg may have thought its bloody streak marked the spot. But it really doesn't matter. That berg, warmed by the Gulf Stream, traveled its fifteen miles per day, continuing its journey, which may have been two thousand miles or more, melting into nothing. A few days later, it was gone.

For all practical purposes, the *Titanic* did the same. It didn't, so far as we know, disintegrate into a countless multitude of water molecules, of course, but it may as well have.

Unless, of course, we can find it.

"*I have a recurring dream. There's this hulk on the camera. It gets closer and I can see details. There it is! R.M.S. Titanic. We found it.*"

—John Jain, scientist from the Scripps Institute of Oceanography

CHAPTER I

THE SEARCH BEGINS

Sixty-nine years after the *Titanic* set sail on her maiden voyage, I found myself going to sea as well. That's about where the similarity ends, however. The ship I was on, the *Gyre*, carried about thirty passengers and crew, while the *Titanic* had a capacity of over three thousand. On the other hand, the *Titanic* had a rather primitive radio—though then it was state of the art—while we carried an extraordinary range of computer, sonar, and other electronic equipment. Of course, things have changed between 1912 and 1981.

One thing that has changed very little indeed is the inherent fascination of the story of the *Titanic*. As a writer, I make my living by telling stories, and the *Titanic's* is one of the greatest ever. It's been told a few times, of course, and very well too. But we were on board to add another chapter to the saga. We wanted to find the great hulk of that great ship, deep in its grave on the ocean floor.

The assignment to write this book came suddenly. With only a few hours notice I traveled to the dock at Woods Hole, Massachusetts, and boarded the *Gyre* at midnight. Although I didn't know it at first, the two men with whom I whiled away the long night of my arrival, which was also the night before we cast off for the North Atlantic, were scientists from the Scripps Institute of Oceanography.

They provided me with my introduction to the story of our trip northward. The year before, a Texas millionaire named Jack Grimm had financed the first summer of the search for the *Titanic*. Fourteen possible target sites for where she might lie were located via sonar images. Unfortunately, the magnetometer, which distinguishes rock from metal, hadn't worked on that trip. The scientists swore that this time it would. This year the expedition also carried sophisticated camera and video equipment that was to be lowered the two and a half miles to the ocean floor to take pictures of the sunken liner.

At 4 A.M. Skip Gleason, one of the Scripps's scientists, was with me in the *Gyre*'s lounge. Gleason resembles a California beach boy, with a daredevil's glint in his eyes. With me already was John Jain, another Scripps scientist. They both share respect, almost adulation, for their boss, Dr. Fred Spiess. Spiess is known in some circles as the father of deep water research, and listening to Jain and Gleason talk, it sounds like he deserves the title.

Spiess earned his Ph.D. from the University of California at Berkeley and is a World War II hero who served on thirteen submarine patrols, an almost unheard-of number, six of them off Japan. He studied under Nobel prize winner Emilio Segre, who himself had been a member of Enrico Fermi's great team in Italy. Spiess has been director of the prestigious Scripps Institution of Oceanography (part of the University of California system) and has earned a roomful of awards and medals. His many patented inventions could have made him rich, had he not devoted his life to research and teaching at a public university.

Among his other inventions Spiess developed FLIP, a research platform three hundred feet long that is towed out to sea, flooded, and tipped vertically. Equipment for studying the ocean floor is suspended from FLIP, which remains virtually still in the water. It has a thousand uses in studying the ocean bottom, not the least being to search for offshore oil.

Fred Spiess, not surprisingly, holds an ultra-secret clearance from the U.S. Navy, and is the recipient of the Conrad, the highest civilian award the Navy can bestow. During his long career he has found dozens of sunken wrecks. He has found previously unknown sea life, discovered hot springs at the bottom of the ocean reaching 600 degrees Fahrenheit, and studied the effects of nuclear waste dumping in the Atlantic. Spiess believes that the ocean holds tremendous future resources for the human race, including food.

The *Gyre* was scheduled to depart at 7 A.M. Jain and Gleason were reminiscing about the previous year's expedition to find the *Titanic*. Its beginning was hardly auspicious. Jack Grimm had arranged for a monkey, named Titan, to accompany the 1980 expedition. The monkey had been taught to point at a spot on the map indicating where the *Titanic* was. Grimm believed this was a remarkable accomplishment that would add immeasurably to the movie he was making about the search. The scientists, especially the illustrious Dr. Spiess, thought the idea bizarre, insane, and circuslike, which could only detract from and hold up to ridicule what they viewed as a very serious endeavor. They laid down the law: it's either us or the monkey.

"Fire the scientists" was Grimm's reply.

Saner heads prevailed. The monkey was left behind, and the scientists found fourteen sonar targets that this year, with luck, would earn them a spot in the record book.

Jain and Gleason also acquainted me with the question of credit, which would continue to be a matter of contention, albeit hidden, throughout the expedition. Grimm certainly would receive it for finding the *Titanic*, but the scientists thought the honor should be their due. It was a dilemma. Without the scientists Grimm could merely enjoy a cruise with his monkey. Without Grimm the scientists would be unable to make the expedition—without funds.

"Schliemann found Troy," Skip Gleason said sensibly. "Why not Jack Grimm finding the *Titanic*? Most scientists wouldn't touch this project with a long fork. It smacks of show business, but we'll learn a lot from this; Spiess knows it, whether we find the ship or not. It would be great to find it. Just great."

At 6:45 A.M. the galley was packed. Most of the feature participants including Dr. Spiess, Dr. William Ryan of Columbia University's Lamont-Doherty Geological Observatory, movie producer Mike Harris, computer whiz Dr. Carl Lowenstein, mechanical genius Tony Boegeman of Scripps, and our captain Don Armand were eating sausage, bacon, and eggs. The food was delicious. If this was a sign of future times, and it was, we were not going to be roughing it.

"Wouldn't you say this is an unusual expedition?" someone asked Armand.

"No. There was bound to be a mother—to go look for the *Titanic* someday."

Jake Vanderkim, a veteran deckhand, did not believe Armand was as nonchalant as he pretended to be. And where going to sea is concerned, Vanderkim would probably speak his mind if he thought a man was wrong even if the person was an admiral. "Well," said Jake, "*I* think the expedition is pretty unusual. No one else has ever done it."

Many members of the crew—Armand himself, if truth were known—had an almost mystical reverence for the most famous ship that ever sank. One of them later said to me, in an almost reverent tone, "More than fifteen hundred people are down there. I think they would want us to come and find them."

Everyone aboard the *Gyre* had a favorite *Titanic* story. Among the others I was told in the course of our journey was the story of Charles Herbert Lightoller, an officer aboard the *Titanic*, a hero who stayed aboard the doomed leviathan until the last moment, then dove overboard and was miraculously spared. "What time did you leave the ship?" a U.S. Senate investigating committee asked Lightoller. "I didn't leave it," was the answer. "Did it leave you?" asked the senator. "Yes sir," came the sad reply.

Then there was the tale of the *Titanic*'s captain, E. J. Smith, who, perhaps negligent at first, went down with his ship as the code of the sea demanded. According to one account, Smith was washed overboard by a powerful wave, and eager hands from a lifeboat reached out to help him. He pulled himself free and swam back to the *Titanic*.

The Unsinkable "Molly" Brown, once and later, a dirt poor mountain girl from Colorado, was "Lady Margaret" that terrible April 15 morning to the many who gave her credit for saving them, as she took charge of the lifeboat in which she floated. John Jacob Astor, New York real estate tycoon, bade his wife good-bye and remained behind.

A mother in steerage suffered the unspeakable: Seven of her ten children perished aboard the *Titanic*.

Maybe the crew member had been right. Maybe, to show people still cared, the mammoth ship should be found.

At eight o'clock we were not yet underway. Captain Armand was still drinking coffee in the galley. People were already restless and wondering why we were still in port.

"Grimm's not here yet," said John Jain.

"Let's go without him," someone suggested.

"He's dead weight," a third agreed, "but there's others like him." This was going to hurt. "Who needs the movie guys? I hear there's even an author aboard. He'll be a big help. And a stuck-up movie star. The Californian, or something like that."

"The Virginian."

"Whatever. We could have more scientists aboard, and fewer dilettantes taking up space."

"What irks me is having to imitate Lord Nelson for a movie cameraman. It's tough enough to . . ."

"Let's go outside," John Jain whispered.

The *Gyre*, though she is 174 feet long and her gross metric tonnage is 297, is registered in Texas as a motorboat because she cannot carry cargo or paying passengers. The *Gyre* is an uncommon motorboat. She is equipped with the most modern technology, more than half of it developed by the U.S. space program, including ultra-sophisticated navigational gear and computers. For our trip the *Gyre* carried 23,000 feet of the strongest steel cable, fitted with a torpedo-shaped device called a fish, which was to be suspended from a crane on the ship's fandeck. The "fish," weighing more than a ton, is then lowered to within twenty meters of the ocean bottom and towed along the floor. The "fish" is essentially a vehicle for the equipment that included the finest side-scan sonar yet developed, sensitive magnetometers, and the camera and color video apparatus to photograph the foundered behemoth. A photograph alone of the *Titanic* would be nearly priceless and would assure the success of any motion picture, but Grimm wanted to go for even bigger game.

If the *Titanic* were definitely found, the millionaire's intention was to commission the *Aluminaut*, a fifty-one-foot submarine owned by Reynolds Metals, to dive on the wreck. The *Aluminaut* is the world's largest privately owned submersible and features nine-foot exterior arms that can reach inside a sunken ship and recover artifacts.

It could be the greatest treasure find in history. Some accounts claim that a fortune in gold bullion and diamonds went down with the *Titanic*. There certainly were countless valuables on board, including a jewel-encrusted copy of the *Rubáiyát of Omar Khayyám*. A jug of wine, a loaf of bread, and thou would not satisfy Grimm. But a considerable fortune would have to be spent first: The *Gyre* alone was costing the tycoon seventy-five hundred dollars a day.

As a newcomer I was eager to explore the *Gyre*, but I was distracted by the clusters of people on the pier below and an excited, anticipatory buzz. Some of those on the pier were easily recognized: reporters with notepads, TV cameramen, wives and children to see off husbands and fathers, tourists curious to see off the ship daring to go in search for the *Titanic*. I decided to mingle on the pier, plenty of time later to check out the *Gyre*.

A short, sturdy man walked up and introduced himself as Bobby Blanco. At age thirty-eight and originally from Cuba, he was a gambler. He enjoyed Las Vegas, Monte Carlo, and big bets on sporting events, but his biggest gamble was finding the *Titanic*. He had lost his job as a restaurant manager when he spent too long in the North Atlantic on the previous year's search. Now he was back for another try, and much of his financial future was at stake. Until I met Bobby I thought Grimm was the only investor. As it turned out, while Grimm was the big investor, there were others, including Nelson Bunker Hunt, the man who once brought mist to the eyes of fellow citizens by lamenting that "a billion dollars isn't what it used to be."

"Grimm knows Bunker Hunt?"

"They're best friends. They go way back. Once they were out in the middle of nowhere late at night with no transportation. No car would pick them up. Grimm told Bunker to lie in the middle of the highway in front of the bus. The bus driver stopped. Luckily or unluckily, if you look at it another way."

Blanco had not been scheduled to come, but had simply showed up in Woods Hole. He was a friend of Mike Harris's, who was producing the movie that was to document the expedition, and he could be valuable to the underwater filmmakers as an expert swimmer, diver, shark fighter, and professional cameraman.

Besides, he had almost all of his money invested in the search, and he wanted to see what was done with it.

Mike Harris vouched for his friend; Bobby agreed to sleep on the *Gyre*'s floor, and Armand relented after having told him there was no room. Everyone liked Bobby, he was a good shipmate, and there was something fascinating about a Cuban Walter Mitty who lived out his dreams.

There was still no sign of Grimm at nine-thirty, and the ranks on the pier had swollen by perhaps fifty percent: most of those aboard the ship had come out on deck to enjoy a beautiful, warm, sunlit Massachusetts morning. The water was glistening green in Nantucket Sound, dotted as far as the eye could see with white sailboats. It could not be this way in the treacherous North Atlantic, although the water had been smooth as glass the morning the *Titanic* went down.

"I'm Dale Chayes," said a bearded, husky young scientist from Columbia University, who had recently spent a great deal of time at sea. Although it became apparent before long that a rivalry existed between the team of scientists from Columbia headed by Dr. William Ryan and the one from Scripps led by Dr. Spiess, both men shared the belief that the best training was not in the classrooms but on the oceans.

Chayes was carrying a copy of the *Boston Herald American* that had a front-page story quoting Jack Grimm: "I think we got that heifer corralled in a box canyon. Now that may sound like Texas idiom, but we've got something down there in a canyon twenty miles long, two miles wide, and two hundred feet deep."

"What do you think?"

"It's hard to tell," said Chayes.

"Is it 'corralled'?"

"The *Titanic* went down in a geologically active area."

"Meaning?"

"It's an interesting area to study."

Dale Chayes, the Columbia scientist, did have one solid piece of misinformation to relay. "I just heard a radio report. It said the *Gyre* is going to tow the *Titanic* to Boston."

Right about then a man of around sixty stopped to talk for a moment. There was no mistaking his identity. Bermuda shorts or no, he was not a tourist taking Polaroid snapshots. He was average height, slim, stood so straight there might have been a board imbedded in his back. Except for a kind face and twinkling eyes, he might have been a Prussian general about to pistol-whip a reluctant recruit. Discipline was the word that came to mind with Dr. Fred Spiess.

"Grimm just arrived in Hyannis," he said. What he seemed to mean was that Grimm would be facing a firing squad, or at least exile to the provinces, if Spiess had his way. It was certain the interaction between the no-nonsense scientist and the eccentric individualistic Texan would be a show all by itself. People not following Spiess's orders were in trouble. Grimm, so the concensus held, took orders from no one. Irresistible force versus immovable object.

"One of the people from Woods Hole has gone to pick him up. We leave at eleven A.M.," he said emphatically.

At 11 A.M. there was still no Jack Grimm, but the reporters and newspeople were toughing it out. They believed the great ship would be found, and it was important they be there at the beginning. The media had passed the time interviewing everyone they could, even the search's most peripheral participants, but they knew the important story was Grimm.

The interview with peripheral people, however, did help establish just how serious the expedition was. It was brought out that the Columbia instrumentation system, developed by Scripps with Grimm's money, also possessed up and down and forward sonar capabilities—not just the side-scan—and the sonar could penetrate *through* the ocean sediment, in case the *Titanic* was

39

buried. This aspect of the design was of utmost importance to the U.S. Navy and Pentagon, committed as they were to improving modern submarine warfare capabilities. Even so, what Grimm was financing as a private citizen might not be developed if it were left to the government.

At 11:15 A.M., four and a quarter hours after the *Gyre* had been set to sail, there was still no sign of the tycoon, but people were willing to talk about him. One of the scientists, feeling more kindly than Dr. Spiess, called him "a searcher for lost legends; you might say he's a genuine romantic, and he would be if there wasn't always the possibility of his making money."

Grimm had financed expeditions to find the Loch Ness monster, Bigfoot, Noah's Ark, and Big Bird (a giant winged creature, probably the imagination of a Texas moonshiner), but the millionaire, considered a genius at locating oil—possessor of perhaps the best record of wells dug to oil found in all of the Southwest—had discovered very little in his Quixotic searches.

"This is different," the scientist said. "What he looked for in the past does not exist. The *Titanic* does."

Speculation was rife on the Woods Hole pier about the condition in which the *Titanic* would be found. Was she now a junk pile bearing no resemblance to the glorious, awesome ship that once humbled and dwarfed everything else on the sea? Or was she rubble strewn across dozens or even hundreds of miles? The mighty 1929 underseas earthquake, more powerful than a hundred hydrogen bombs, had severed transatlantic cables as it rumbled along the ocean bottom. The quake, as scientists speculated, might have broken the ship into a million pieces, or buried her, or moved her very far from her original resting place.

Yet she might be remarkably preserved, since at that depth no sunlight and virtually no oxygen are present, and the water temperature is constant. It was also possible that the bodies of the people trapped inside might be preserved.

As I ruminated on these bits of information, I noticed a slight movement—nothing more—off to the right. I heard several muffled sounds of recognition, and a general drift of people in the direction of the noise. Spiess, near the gangplank, had murder in his eyes.

The object of attention was just under six feet tall and had graying hair, thick, bushy eyebrows, and dark, darting eyes. His demeanor seemed to be satisfied and mischievous but with the controlled urgency of "a man with hounds at his heels," as he was once described.

At Grimm's elbow was a handsome hulk jauntily sporting a beret that seemed to have been made from a bath towel. He had a readily recognizable face: it belonged to James Drury, the Virginian himself, star of the nine-year hit series of the same name. Drury was a bona fide TV star, but he was not what the reporters wanted. The press of bodies was all up against Grimm.

Grimm was very good in front of the cameras. If the interviewers expected a braggadocio Texan they were sorely disappointed. The millionaire was thoughtful, spoke quietly, knew more about the *Titanic*—so it appeared—than the scientists who were supposed to find her. Why did that seem unusual? The rich man had become rich by studying science, taking a degree in geology at the University of Oklahoma. "Not a bit of luck in this business, boys, no ESP, just solid homework." His money, regardless of tax deductions, had been bet on finding the ship. But more important to Grimm, I later learned, was pressure from peers: he had convinced friends to invest in finding the *Titanic*, some of whom had made fortunes investing in his tips on oil wells, and it was a matter of honor and pride and *personal standing* that he be successful.

Sidling from interview to interview, he told Boston's Channel 7: "We have highly technical equipment, and unless we're looking in the wrong area, and I don't believe we are, we'll find her."

"The scientists we have are the best in the world," Grimm told another interviewer. "The *Titanic* is lost and we're going to try to find her."

"You're in this for the money," a particularly aggressive young radio reporter asserted.

"Partly."

"You're looking for oil," said another.

"The search for the *Titanic* is just a cover."

"No."

That was what many aboard the *Gyre* feared, that it was just a search for oil, damn finding the ship.

Then Grimm started up the gangplank. A foghorn blew three times; the engine started, and the *Gyre* moved sideways from the dock. Then she went slowly backward to point her nose through Vineyard Sound to Nantucket Sound and out to the Atlantic. It was 12:34. People on the pier were taking movies.

It soon became clear that the galley was the place to be to understand what was going on. Late in the afternoon, Grimm and Lamont-Doherty scientist John Farre sat talking about the expedition. Farre was earning his doctorate in geology and had a zest for field work, making him Dr. Ryan's star pupil. He was also tall, handsome, and authoritative. Once when Jack Grimm attempted to sneak off the watch he had been assigned three minutes early (there was a poker game in the galley, and the tycoon was eager for action), Farre had laid into him.

"What the hell is this!" screamed the twenty-four-year-old, seeming to rise to the height of giants. "Sit down, Grimm! You've got three minutes to go!"

Grimm, looking like a naughty child, had sat back down.

Farre wanted to find the *Titanic*, but like all of the scientists he also had other considerations. This was an opportunity to study the ocean floor, perhaps gain insight into underwater landslides, do environmental tests, and if the ship were found, the chance to investigate the deterioration caused by sixty-nine years on the ocean bottom. Someday people may have to live in the ocean (perhaps with artificially made gills) and the scientists were aware their findings could help make that future possible.

But Grimm didn't want to hear it. The scientists were using his money, he felt, to further their own ambitions. They really didn't care about the *Titanic*. There was logic to this suggestion until the scientists themselves were encountered, and then it evaporated. The child who was in all of them felt it would be wonderful if they could find the lost ship.

Nor was Grimm looking for tax dodges, or oil, though he would take it if he found it. He knew more about the *Titanic* than anyone aboard the *Gyre*, and his eyes sparkled when he talked about her. "She wasn't unique," he was saying. "She had a twin sister, the *Olympic*, and when the *Titanic* gave her CQD, the *Olympic* was five hundred miles away going in the opposite direction. The *Olympic* came charging to the rescue but she was too late."

The *Titanic* story was so fantastic it was not surprising it could hook even a hard-headed businessman like Grimm. He talked about the prescient 1898 novel, *Titan*, written by Morgan Robertson. "It told of a giant luxury liner eight hundred feet long. Get this," he instructed. "The fictional *Titan* was supposed to be unsinkable. It was packed with rich passengers, hit an iceberg on her maiden voyage in April, and sank in the Atlantic. Almost everyone died because there were too few lifeboats, just like the *Titanic*."

Was there a curse on the *Titanic*? Ever since the sinking reports had circulated of a mysterious Black Buddha carried in *Titanic* Captain Smith's safe. The statue was supposed to be encrusted with very rare gems. The story holds that it was stolen from a temple in Peking and had attached to it a curse that doomed the White Star liner. Grimm did not believe in the curse, but the Black Buddha might be very real.

"Then there might be a curse on us," said Jake Vanderkim. "We might go down just like the *Titanic*. There would be a way to be famous."

Some twenty people who survived the *Titanic* disaster are still alive; time has not dimmed their memories. Frank Goldsmith (Mike Harris located him) was eleven years old and half a mile away in a lifeboat when the luxury liner shuddered for the final time, rose almost perpendicular, and knifed through the glass smooth black water on her final thirteen-thousand-foot trip to the bottom. Goldsmith lives in Detroit, near Tiger Stadium. "I'm close enough to the ballpark," he recalls, "to hear the roar of the crowd when a home run is hit. The noise always reminds me, although it is different, of the screams of those on the *Titanic* when she disappeared."

Thirty people were aboard the *Gyre* as she sailed through Vineyard Sound, but a hundred or a thousand times that number had wanted to come along. When it was revealed that the 1981 search would take up where the 1980 left off, there was a deluge of requests to accompany the expedition. No fewer than fifty marine engineers wrote with plans explaining how the *Titanic* could be raised, which of course was patently impossible given the current state of technology. An entire third grade class in Denver asked if they could be part of the voyage. Numerous young women, scantily clad and promising to do "anything," sent pictures of themselves. No fewer than twenty-eight psychics "knew" where the *Titanic* rested, and each gave a different location. An elderly man claimed he should be included on the search because he knew more about the White Star liner than anyone else alive. How did he acquire this knowledge? "I made four round-trip crossings on her before she went down."

Most of the correspondents were sincere people captivated by the legend of the *Titanic* and eager to share in the adventure of finding her. To *recover* something from the ship would be ecstasy beyond imagination. (Later, at a fund-raising charity affair, Jack

Grimm auctioned a *one-inch* thread from one of the *Titanic*'s carpets and it brought two thousand dollars. A strip of the carpet had been removed by one of the workmen before the ship sailed, found its way to the California State Historical Society, and was in turn given to Grimm in acknowledgment of his efforts to find the *Titanic*.)

The idea of finding the *Titanic* had originated with Harris, and he had persuaded Grimm to put together the team of investors whose money made the expedition possible. Harris is a member of the exclusive Explorers Club of New York and he had carried the Club's flag on the 1980 search. His documentary films on such wide ranging topics as radiation-ridden Bikini Lagoon and searches for Noah's Ark had won him awards, respect, and recognition.

One of his most recent efforts was the chronicle of the 1980 expedition, which features Orson Welles as the on-camera narrator. He was certain that they had found the *Titanic* in one of the fourteen targets. I asked him what he would do if we didn't find it this trip.

"I'll probably kill myself."

"They sauntered past the line of white-painted lifeboats hanging in the davits—anachronisms, these, some people may have thought; since the Titanic, as everyone knew, was unsinkable."

—Geoffrey Marcus,
The Maiden Voyage

CHAPTER II

LIFE ABOARD THE *TITANIC*

The *Titanic* was conceived one evening after dinner. In 1907 Lord Pirrie, Chairman of Harland & Wolff, and his wife entertained Mr. & Mrs. J. Bruce Ismay at the Pirries' London house. After dinner while the ladies left the men to their port and cigars, Ismay, as Managing Director of the White Star Line and Chairman of International Mercantile Marine Co., the conglomerate backed by J. Pierpont Morgan, and Lord Pirrie (Thomas Andrews's uncle) drew rough sketches.

The plan was for a service of luxurious liners designed to overwhelm Cunard and Hamburg-American Lines for the transatlantic trade. Competition was fierce in 1907. German ships had increasingly cut into the customarily British trade. That year the German challenge had been met by Cunard, who launched the *Lusitania* and the *Mauretania*, the largest and fastest ships in the world, but the White Star Line was not about to be left out of the running. They were already well placed, having recently gained an advantage by altering their New York–bound shipping routes from Southampton by stopping at Cherbourg. Americans traveling in Europe or spending seasons in London, Paris, or on the Côte d'Azur were thus easily served.

Ismay and Pirrie's plan was to build three immense sister ships that would offer the fashionably rich, mostly American trade the same spacious and comfortable accommodation as a first-class hotel. The service would be regular and guarantee a week's crossing on the safest and most comfortable ships afloat. The ships would carry the latest in technology, and their decorations and appointments would be drawn from the best of past and present civilizations. Grand plans indeed were concocted that night.

Work began almost immediately on the first two ships. Blueprints were drawn; backers were found, and construction was underway within a year. Among the details to be arranged for were special building requirements. Since the first two ships were to be constructed at the same time, special twin slips were built to hold them. They were to be so large that a special crane had to be bought. Harland & Wolff had to expand and make new space for enlarged boiler, joiner, and plating shops. The docks in New York were extended. Getting permission for this was no mean feat, but then J. P. Morgan could exert more pressure than most. It was financed by the New York taxpayers.

The *Olympic* was finished first. On May 31, 1911, she set sail on her maiden voyage from Southampton, carrying among her notable passengers J. Bruce Ismay. He made the voyage to check out her appointments and structure, and suggest improvements for the perfected vessel to come, the *Titanic*.

On the same day the *Titanic* was launched on her fitting out trials from Belfast. Among the notables present for her launching was J. Pierpont Morgan, who made a special trip to be there. He was given a tour of the ship, and shown where his special quarters were to be built (they were known as one of the two Millionaire's Suites). Much of her vast interior was yet to be completed, but by

April of the following year the *Titanic* would steam to Southampton, measuring 883 feet long and 92 feet wide and weighing 46,328 tons, fractionally longer and heavier than her sister ship.

The world eagerly awaited the *Titanic*'s maiden voyage. The *Olympic* had instantly proved popular, so popular that she needed more first-class accommodation, for her proportions were vast, her appointments luxurious, and her service impeccable—she was a floating advertisement for the even more wonderful ship being readied. The *Titanic* was ballyhooed on both sides of the Atlantic. Scientific, technical, and engineering journals marveled. The magazine *Engineering* devoted a special issue to the *Titanic*, while the staid journal *The Shipbuilder* claimed that the *Olympic* and *Titanic* together were the rightful heirs to the Victorian dream, the appropriate melding of nineteenth-century ideals with twentieth-century technology.

The popular press hailed her as "The Wonder Ship," "The Millionaire's Special," "The Biggest Ship in the World," "The Last Word in Luxury," and "The Unsinkable Ship." One of her passengers later wrote, "The world had waited expectantly for its launching and again for its sailing; had read accounts of its tremendous size and unexampled completeness and luxury; had felt it a matter of the greatest satisfaction that such a comfortable, and above all such a safe boat had been designed and built—the unsinkable lifeboat."

As a naked ship, before being fitted out with her internal modifications and decoration, she was a marvel. She stood nine decks, or eleven stories high. If stood on her end, as popular advertisements showed her, she was taller than the new Woolworth Building in New York, which was a mere 750 feet high. Her four funnels, three for discharging steam and smoke and a dummy for ventilation, were each 22 feet in diameter and rose 62 feet above their casings. Twin locomotive engines could drive through each one with room to spare on each side. Her boilers provided the power (over 50,000 horsepower) to move the vessel at over 23

51

knots or 26 miles per hour. They also provided power for evaporation and refrigeration plants as well as four passenger elevators, a 50-telephone switchboard for ship use, and a 5-kilowatt wireless telegraph station.

Her power plants were a combination of two reciprocating engines and one low-pressure turbine. She was the first ship fitted with a Parsons turbine, which gave increased power without increasing the steam consumption. The reciprocating engines drove the two outside screws and the turbine the middle propeller. Twenty-nine boilers and one hundred fifty-nine furnaces provided her power.

Her hull was divided into sixteen "watertight" compartments, divided by fifteen transverse bulkheads. The bulkheads ran from the bottom of the ship up five decks fore and aft and four decks amidships, well above the water level. Her steel bottom was double-skinned and reinforced with tons of concrete.

She was fitted with sixteen 30-foot lifeboats fitted into double-acting davits which were designed to hold two or three times the number of boats. She also carried four collapsible lifeboats.

The rudder which guided her into Southampton almost a year later on April 3, 1912, weighed 101 tons, and the three anchors which brought her to rest weighed over 30 tons.

White Star had taken great pains to make her maiden voyage something special. They had gathered the best officers in their fleet for the historic passage. Captain E. J. Smith, commodore of the line, took command, coming from the *Olympic* for one last voyage before retiring. Known to all as E. J., Smith was respected and liked, popular both with those who served under him and those he served. He was a big man with full, white whiskers who looked bluff and hearty, though his voice was quiet, his temper even, and his smile ready. According to Second Officer C. H. Lightoller, "He was a great favorite, and a man any officer would have given his ears to sail under."

Smith brought with him H. T. Wilde as Chief Officer, also from the *Olympic*. This slightly upset the order of the officers already on board, causing Chief Officer William Murdoch to drop to First, First Officer Lightoller to drop to Second, and Second Officer Davy Blair to be bumped from the trip. Blair was bitterly disappointed at the time, for it was considered a plum to be assigned to the *Titanic*. Purser McElroy and Ship Surgeon O'Loughlin were also venerable employees, and especially popular with passengers.

Of the rest of the officers and crew, few had experienced a ship anywhere near as large as the *Titanic*. "It is difficult to convey the size of a ship like the *Titanic*," wrote Lightoller, "when you could actually walk miles along decks and passages covering different ground all the time. . . . It took me fourteen days before I could with confidence find my way from one part of that ship to another."

As they assembled, everyone had to adjust to the ship's vastness, from the crew of nearly 400 (officers to greasers) to the hotel staff of 518 who looked after every detail of shipboard life, from keeping the quarters and public rooms to providing musical entertainment to manning the hospital and dining rooms. The first impressions must have been of wonder at how large, spacious, luxurious, and well-equipped she was. The firemen prepared to stoke over 650 tons of coal into the furnaces each day, while the stewards and stewardesses would care for up to 2,433 passengers.

Preparing any ship for commission is an arduous task. "With the *Titanic* it was night and day work," Lightoller recalled, "organizing here, receiving stores there, arranging duties, trying and testing out the different contrivances."

Several days before sailing, the Board of Trade representative came to inspect, checking to make sure all regulations were met. Lifeboats were examined; life-saving equipment tested, emergency rockets, flares, and lights approved. The inspector, known for his thoroughness, closely scrutinized hundreds of things. The *Titanic* met or exceeded all the regulations.

An even more rigorous examination was conducted by Thomas Andrews. During the final week he supervised the final preparations. He showed the ship owners around, and interviewed engineers, officials, agents, managers, and subcontractors. He settled squabbles among the staff and was called in to fix or attend to countless details. When something needed doing, Andrews was the one people called for. His secretary wrote that Andrews personally "put in their place such things as racks, tables, chairs, berth ladders, electric fans, saying that except he saw everything right he could not be satisfied."

As always, he was the dutiful husband, writing daily to his wife. While in one letter he wrote about the technicalities of cofferdams and submerged cylinders on the propeller boss, to his wife he also wrote, "The *Titanic* is now about complete and will I think do the old firm credit tomorrow when we sail."

At last the ship was ready, and Southampton hotels were full of passengers ready to board. Lightoller observed that "from end to end, the ship, which for several days had been like a nest of bees, now resembled a hive about to swarm."

On the morning of April 10, 1912, the hive swarmed to welcome its charges. Of those already on board, Andrews, as usual, was one of the busiest, having come on board at 6 A.M. to make a long final inspection before sailing.

Another early arrival on the scene was J. Bruce Ismay, making the maiden voyage to conduct his own inspection and evaluation. Ismay had taken over the White Star Line when his father, the company's founder, had died thirteen years earlier. Ismay the younger had already earned the reputation of a shrewd and able autocrat and disciplinarian. Under his leadership the company handsomely increased its profits and was about to sprint ahead of Cunard in the race for supremacy. He was a man to be respected, but he was difficult to like.

Ismay's suggestions following his trip on the maiden voyage of the *Olympic* had produced a number of changes for the *Titanic*. Part of one deck had been made into cabins for one hundred more first-class passengers. A forward promenade deck had been enclosed in glass to protect passengers from harsh weather.

Ismay showed off the ship to his wife and three children, who had come to see him off. Entering the ornate grand staircase, they could see the great clock at the stairhead, flanked by two bronze figures, one of Honor, the other Glory. One flight up to the Boat Deck they saw the gymnasium fitted with all the latest exercise equipment from Wiesbaden and the first miniature golf course. The elevators down took them to the swimming pool (heated) and the regulation squash court, seven decks below. Perhaps they even peeked in at the fully equipped darkroom provided for passengers interested in developing their own film.

As the morning progressed the ship filled. People seemed to be settling in before sailing. Two Americans felt at home enough to wage a battle of the rackets on the squash court fully an hour before sailing time. Passengers continued to board, some having just arrived on the Boat Train from London. Perhaps the most notable was the flamboyant John Jacob Astor and his bride Madeline. They had spent the winter in Egypt, escaping the New York social scene that had thoroughly snubbed them on their marriage the previous fall. New York society had accepted Astor's divorce from his first wife in 1909, but they would not accept his new marriage. His plans for introducing his bride into society and perhaps grooming her to take his late mother's place as social leader had fallen flat. More than one passenger hoped to catch a glimpse of the man worth $150 million and his young, expectant wife.

On boarding they went directly to one of the two Millionaire's Suites. These suites were fitted and decorated to suit the needs and tastes of the ultra rich. They were not merely luxurious staterooms, but apartments consisting of a spacious parlor, two bedrooms, and a bathroom complete with every modern convenience. They were decorated with French and English antiques, thick carpeting, and rich upholstery. They were heated not by radiators, but by grates delivering heat from a coal burner. Windows replaced portholes and an Elizabethan style half-timbered private promenade deck kept residents from having to rub shoulders with other first-class passengers.

The other Millionaire Suite was to have been occupied by J. P. Morgan, who had booked passage but at the last moment was forced to go to Aix because of illness. Henry Clay Frick, who was closely connected with Andrew Carnegie, Morgan's rival, was booked too but cancelled. Lord Pirrie was supposed to make the trip, but was forced to cancel because of his health. They were the lucky ones.

Important Americans who boarded the *Titanic* included Benjamin Guggenheim, member of the successful commercial family and the man responsible for expanding the American smelting industry. George Widener, son and right-hand man to P.A.B. Widener, the Philadelphia streetcar magnate, was traveling with his wife and their son, Harry, a noted rare-book collector. Mr. and Mrs. Isidor Straus were returning from a restful winter on the Riviera. Straus had emigrated from Bavaria as a boy and over the years amassed a fortune, primarily in banking. With his brother Nathan and R. H. Macy he had built the famous New York department store. He had also served a term in Congress and was a friend of President Grover Cleveland.

Most of the first- and second-class passengers had come down from London. Americans were fascinated with the sparkle, grace, and ceremony of a London season, though Anglo-American marriages between the rich and the titled had already peaked (perhaps the most famous issue of one of these marriages was Winston Churchill).

Promptly at noon, a siren signaled that the largest ship in the world was sailing. Though there was no official ceremony to mark the occasion, save the lilting airs provided by the ship's orchestra, people crowded the *Titanic*'s decks waving, shouting, and whistling to loved ones on shore as the great ship slipped her moorings and glided away from her berth.

Colonel Archibald Gracie and Mr. and Mrs. Straus stood chatting as the ship moved along until they heard what sounded like pistol shots ring out. It was not a pistol, but the passenger ship *New York* breaking her mooring lines. The suction caused by the tremendous displacement of water as the *Titanic* passed had pulled the smaller ship closer and closer.

The *Titanic's* master instantly shut down the engines, but the *New York* moved perilously close before tugs were able to gently move her away. As they stood watching Mr. Straus recalled how he had made the maiden voyage on the *New York* when she was considered the most advanced ship on the seas.

Others on deck were excited by the incident too. Second-class passenger Lawrence Beesley remembered a young cinematograph photographer who "followed the whole scene with eager eyes, turning the handle of his camera with the most evident pleasure as he recorded the unexpected incident on his films."

Underway once more, the *Titanic* moved slowly out to the channel, past the lawns of the Royal Yacht Squadron, past the Isle of Wight, and into the English Channel. The next stop was to be Cherbourg by early evening.

Entering the first-class dining room on D Deck through the white paneled Jacobean reception room, first-class passengers soon sat down to their first of many luxurious meals, an elegant luncheon. Strains of music from the orchestra were to be heard in the background. The room was immense, spanning the entire width of the ship, and could comfortably seat five hundred and fifty. The lighting was recessed behind cathedral windows and gave a continuous soft daylight glow to the entirely white room. Those wishing a private meal could request seating in one of the many recessed bays.

The second-class dining room was impressive as well. While not as grand as first class, it too ran the breadth of the ship and was comfortable and pleasant. Even the third-class dining room was comfortable, partly because it was located in the center of the ship where motion was to be felt least. And though the food served there was not in the grand style of the first and second classes, it was well prepared and plentiful—a true bargain at the modest cost of the passage.

The kitchens that provided the food were the most modern found anywhere. In fact, they were a popular tourist attraction, as cooks demonstrated the machines that sliced, peeled, chopped, beat, warmed, cooled, cooked, and froze. The automatic potato peeler was one of the additions suggested by Mr. Ismay. There were huge walk-in refrigerators devoted solely to fish, game, poultry, dairy foods, and vegetables. There was a walk-in freezer that held only ice cream. There were even refrigerators for cut flowers and fruits to be given as gifts, and bottled mineral waters.

After luncheon passengers dispersed to various activities. Perhaps the most common was seeing the sights of the ship or trying to. Even aided by guidebooks and electric signs many lost their way, including crewmen. Lightoller later recalled that it took three fellow officers an entire day to find a huge gangway, one large enough for a horse and cart to be driven through, had there been one on board.

Many tourists began at the sumptuous domed grand staircase. It was with good reason that they took it up to the Boat Deck and found the gymnasium. T. W. McCawley, a genial man of tireless enthusiasm, held forth, kindly urging people to try out the mechanical camel and horse, and demonstrating the bicycle racing, rowing, and boxing machines.

Other popular stops included not only the swimming pool and squash court, but the exotic Turkish bath, complete with gilded cooling rooms and Maude Slocombe, a full-time masseuse. Even the sick bay was a sight to see, for on this ship it was a complete, well-staffed, modern hospital.

Passengers not lucky enough to have their own private promenade deck strolled down the plentiful public ones. Many looked in on the veranda and palm court, thoughtfully enclosed and outfitted with comfortable furniture and tables placed amidst gracious potted palms.

The second-class library on C Deck quickly became a gathering point for the solid middle class. Decorated in mahogany with functional white fluted columns, it was beautifully furnished with sofas, armchairs, card tables, and writing bureaus and tables. The books were housed in glass cases along one wall. Children played in the corridor outside, quickly establishing it as their domain. Among them were two toddlers traveling with their doting father, who called himself Hoffman. He said he was taking them to visit relatives in the States. Actually his name was Navatril, and he had kidnapped them from his wife in Nice. Later, when the children were saved, worldwide coverage was used to discover their mother.

Even the third class had commodious public rooms and open spaces. Compared to the villages most of the emigrants knew, life on the *Titanic* was a luxurious vacation. Men and women slept in separate quarters, but those quarters were clean, well lit, and spacious. Their common room housed one of the ship's fifteen pianos, and their recreation deck provided continuous entertainment. One of the few complaints heard was that the smoking room was at the opposite end of the ship from the quarters, necessitating a good hike and back for the sake of a smoke or a hand of cards.

While passengers familiarized themselves with the ship, stewards had placed deck chairs out, signaling the start of normal ship routine. Tea service followed. The *Titanic* was well and truly under way, in the great mammoth tradition of British service and steamship.

By early evening the *Titanic* reached Cherbourg, where she would take on most of the rest of her monied passengers. A special train had come from Paris that afternoon, bringing with it members of the spring exodus from the Riviera. Most, needless to say, were rich Americans.

Once again, the passengers who came aboard represented power as well as wealth. Among them were Charles Melville Hays, President of the Canadian Grand Trunk Railway. He had been abroad studying hotels, gathering ideas for the hotels he was establishing along his line. John B. Thayer, a Vice President of the Pennsylvania Railroad, boarded with his wife and teenage son. The Arthur Ryersons, an important steel family, boarded with their three children, governess, and maid.

Perhaps the most colorful to board was Mrs. J. J. Brown, later immortalized in the musical *The Unsinkable Molly Brown*. The wife of a Colorado mine manager who struck it rich in 1894, Mrs. Brown had embarked on a life of high living. When she and her husband were snubbed by Denver society she moved to Newport, Rhode Island, where her exuberant "diamond in the rough" character was more appreciated. Estranged from her husband, who found he didn't care for the millionaire's life and stayed in Denver, she entertained lavishly and traveled the world in grand style. She was returning from a full winter season abroad, part of it spent with the Astors in Egypt.

Sir Cosmo and Lady Duff Gordon also embarked at Cherbourg. They too, were a noted couple, for Lady Duff Gordon, a sister of Elinor Glyn, had established a couture house called Madame Lucile, after herself. Her enterprise had proved so fashionable and successful that by 1912 she employed over a thousand workers and had branches in Paris, London, and New York. For this trip she and her husband were traveling as merely Mr. and Mrs. Brown.

Almost as soon as the ship left Cherbourg, an elegant dinner was served in the first-class dining room. The ship's French restaurant (another innovation) had her complement of a la carte diners. The restaurant, decorated in Louis Seize style of muted colors and rich appointments, was equipped to serve private parties and provided service at any time of the day or night, allowing passengers more freedom than normal shipboard service had to offer. The Cafe Parisien outside the restaurant provided the illusion of a French sidewalk cafe. Complete with trellis and clinging vines, it soon proved a popular meeting place for the younger set.

After dinner the evening's entertainment got underway. The ship's orchestra gave a concert on the promenade as patrons had their coffee and liqueur in the palm court and listened. Colonel Archibald Gracie recalled one such evening:

> . . . according to usual custom, we adjourned to the palm room, with many others, for the usual coffee at individual tables where we listened to the always delightful music of the *Titanic*'s band. On the occasion, full dress was always *en régle*; and it was a subject both of observation and admiration, that there were so many beautiful women—then especially in evidence—aboard the ship.

After the concert a number of the men repaired to the first-class smoking room for the nightly ritual of cigars, cards, and conversation. They formed groups in the large room: bilingual bridge games began in one section, poker games in another.

Among the regulars, Major Archibald Butt, President Taft's military aide, led one group in political conversation. He had just returned from Rome, where he had gone to rest at the urging of his friend Frank Millet. Butt was caught in the middle of a tug of war between President Taft and former President Theodore Roosevelt, both of whom he was close to. His conversation was always topical and interesting. Millet, the painter and poet, held forth in another group, where the discussion was of travel—upcoming and past—painting, and literature.

Perhaps the most popular conversationalist of all in the smoking room was W. T. Stead, the English journalist. Nearing the end of a long and influential career, Stead could look back on some landmark accomplishments. He had exhibited almost unequalled political and social power in England. A tough but charismatic man, he introduced the press interview into British journalism. He helped bring about the Naval Defence Act, and exposed white slave trade and helped pass legislation against it. In recent years he had taken up spiritualism to the embarrassment of some of his colleagues. He was on his way to New York at the invitation of President Taft, to attend a special peace conference at Carnegie Hall.

As the evening drew to a close, the ship's passengers retired for the night. So too did much, but certainly not all, of the ship. Like the running of any hotel or sailing ship, the work continued around the clock. Shifts of workers proceeded as normal. Down in the hold, the furnaces were hungry. In the kitchens, the night bakery was busy making the morning's bread and rolls. Hallways and public rooms were scrubbed, and navigation proceeded, taking the ship toward Queenstown, Ireland, for her last stop before sailing across the Atlantic to New York.

The *Titanic* arrived at Queenstown at noon on April 11. Most of the passengers coming on board were young Irish emigrants, traveling third class. Leaving behind family and friends forever, they joined the international group already aboard. All told there were 709 people traveling steerage, and they came from the British Isles, Scandinavia, the Mediterranean, the Far East, and the Middle East.

While at Queenstown, the press was, as usual, invited aboard. At every stop the press had swarmed the major sights, taking notes and, so the White Star Line hoped, returned to their offices to file glowing reports. So far, line officials had been delighted with the coverage.

The *Titanic* had not docked at Queenstown but was moored in the harbor. There she received her passengers, from tenders that drew alongside. Everything proceeded smoothly, except for one small incident. One of the stokers thought it a good joke to climb up the dummy funnel and peer out for the benefit of those below. The sight of a black figure emerging from the stack was not appreciated at all, but considered a bad omen to many of those in the tender alongside.

The weather was perfect as the ship steamed along the Irish coast and out to the open sea. Shipboard life once again settled into its pleasurable routine of meals, relaxation, and entertainment. The sea was so calm that very few fell ill. "Each morning the sun rose behind us in a sky of circular clouds, stretching round the horizon in long, narrow streaks, and rising tier upon tier above the skyline, red and pink and fading from pink to white, as the sun rose higher in the sky," remembered Lawrence Beesley.

After breakfast passengers settled down to serious relaxation. Some used the sports facilities; others took their exercise walking the miles of decks or playing shuffleboard. Many eschewed exercise of any kind and took to the deck chairs on the sheltered promenades where they soaked in the sun, read, wrote letters, or sat staring out to sea. Stewards brought them warming cups of broth and hot chocolate. Some people preferred having their coffee in the Cafe Parisien, while others chose the quiet of the libraries for reading, writing, chatting, and playing cards. The ship's orchestra almost always seemed to be giving a concert. One young Scotsman continually practiced his bagpipes on the third-class deck.

Not everyone had the luxury to watch the sun rise or spend a leisurely day. One of the busiest places was the ship's Marconi station, where possibly the ship's two hardest workers, Jack Phillips and Harold Bride, sent the marconigrams. Wireless telegraphy was still an innovation aboard ship, but in the ten years since Guglielmo Marconi had patented his magnetic detector, it had revolutionized communication. In the past a ship at sea was cut off from the mainland and from all other ships until it landed, but with a wireless station ships could communicate with each other and with land based stations. It proved vital as both an emergency network and a news source.

The *Titanic*'s maiden voyage was greeted with quantities of messages. For three days Phillips and Bride worked feverishly taking and sending personal marconigrams. Twice a day there was also a newscast broadcast from Cape Cod, Massachusetts, and Poldhu, from which the ship's daily newspaper compiled its current affairs page. Stock prices as well were quoted. Given the men of business who frequented the luxury liners, the shipboard wireless telegraphy was soon found to be an indispensable business tool. In addition, the wireless was a popular novelty for passengers to send personal messages. Colonel Gracie reported that Mr. and Mrs. Straus were excited by the prospect of sending a telegram to their son and daughter-in-law on a passing liner.

All told, everyone seemed pleased with the *Titanic* and her progress. Passengers almost unanimously agreed she was the most stable and comfortable ship they had ever sailed on; the officers seemed pleased with her progress. As she left Queenstown it appeared the *Titanic* would make the maiden voyage as triumphantly as the world expected. Lawrence Beesley described his feelings as the last sight of land slipped away:

> . . . the coast rounded away from us to the northwest, and the last we saw of Europe was the Irish mountains dim and faint in dropping darkness. With the thought that we had seen the last of land until we set foot on the shores of America, I retired to the library to write letters, little knowing that many things would happen to us all—many experiences sudden, vivid, and impressive to be encountered; many perils to be faced; many good and true people for whom we should have to mourn—before we saw land again.

Titanic

Captain E.J. Smith

Upper deck of the *Titanic*, looking forward

Gymnasium of the *Titanic*

Reading room of the *Titanic*

Main stairway of the *Titanic*, Top E deck

CARGO OF TITANIC VALUED AT $420,000

Merchandise of Every Kind Went to the Bottom with Giant Liner.

ALL HIGH-CLASS FREIGHT

Tiffany, Claflin, Lazard Brothers, the Barings, and the Express Companies Among the Consigners.

The full list of the freight and express cargo on the White Star liner Titanic when that vessel went down last Monday morning was received in New York Friday in the registered mail of the Cunarder Mauretania. The manifest shows a cargo the value of which is conservatively estimated at about $420,000.

The weight of the cargo was about 1,400 tons, not a large amount, all things considered, until it is remembered that cargo was a secondary matter so far as the Titanic was concerned. That ship was built for high-priced passengers and what little cargo she carried was also of the kind that demanded quick transportation. The Titanic's freight was for the most part what is known as high-class package freight.

Among the consignees of the Titanic's cargo were Tiffany & Co., whose consignment was silver goods; H. B. Claflin Company, Baring Brothers Company, the American Express Company, the United States Express Company, Lazard Freres, Austin Nichols & Co., Acker, Merrall & Condit Co., Alfred Suter, A. G. Spalding & Bro., the Spencerian Pen Company, B. Altman & Co., F. R. Arnold & Co., Adams Express Company, and Wells-Fargo Express Company.

The manifest of the Titanic follows, the name of the consignee coming first and the nature and amount of the goods consigned following:

Wakem & McLaughlin—1 ca wine.
Thorer & Praetorius—3 bls skins.
Carter, W. E.—1 ca auto.
Fuchs & Lang Mfg. Co.—4 cs printers' blankets.
Spalding, A. G., & Bro.—36 cs athletic goods.
Park & Tilford—1 ca tooth paste, 5 cs drug sundries, 1 case brushware.
Maltus & Ware—8 cs orchids.
Spencerian Pen Co.—4 cs pens.
Sherman Sons & Co.—7 cs cottons.
Claflin, H. B., Co.—12 cs cotton laces.
Muser Bros.—4 cs tissues.
Isler & Guye—4 bls straw.
Hyldenan & Leamer—1 cse tulle.
Petry, F. H., & Co.—1 cse tulle.
Metzger, A. S.—2 cs tulle.
Mills & Gibbs—29 cs cottons, 1 cse gloves.
Field, Marshall, & Co.—1 cse gloves.
N. Y. Motion Picture Co.—1 cse films.
Thorburn, J. M., & Co.—3 cs bulbs.
Rawnick & H. Trad. Co.—28 bgs sticks.
Dujardin & Ladnuck—10 bxs melons.
Amer. Exp. Co.—25 cs. mdse.
Tiffany Co.—1 cask china, 1 cse silver goods.
Lustig Bros.—4 cs straw hats.
Kuyper, P. C., & Co.—1 cse elastic cords, 1 cse leather.
Cohen, M., Bros.—5 pgs skins.
Gross, Engel Co.—3 cs skins.
Wilson, P. K., & Son—61 cs tulle.
Salin Textile Co.—1 cse lace goods.
Calhoun, Robbins & Co.—1 cse cotton laces, ½ cse brushware.
Victor & Achelis—1 cse brushware.
Baumgarten, Wm., & Co.—2 cs furniture.
Spielman Co.—2 cs silk crape.
Northughani Lace Works—2 cs cottons.
Naday & Fleischer—1 cse laces.
Rosenthal, Leo J., Co.—4 cs cottons.
Wakem & McLaughlin—25 cs biscuits, 42 cs ———

Loewing, T., & C.—7 cs biscuits.
Crown Perfumes Co.—3 cs soap perfume.
Meadows, T., & Co.—4 cs books, 3 bxs samples, 1 cs parchments.
Thomas & Pierson—2 cs hardware, 2 cs furniture.
American Express Co.—1 cse elastics, 1 cse gramaphone, 1 cs hosiery, 5 cs books, 1 cse canvas, 1 cse rubber goods, 2 cs prints, 5 cs films, 1 cse tweed, 1 cs aero fittings, a quantity of oak beams, 1 cse plants, 1 cse speedometer, 1 pge effects, 2 cs sample, 8 cs pasta, 2 cs camera and stand, 4 cs books.
Sheldon, G. W., & Co.—1 cse machinery.
Maltus & Ware—15 cs alarm apparatus, 11 cs orchids.
Hempstead & Sons—30 cs plants.
Braach & Rothenstein—2 cs lace collars, 2 cs books.
Isler & Guye—53 pkgs straw.
Baring Brothers & Co.—48 cs rubber, 100 bgs galls.
Altman, B., & Co.—1 cse cottons.
Stern, S.—60 cs salt powder.
Arnold, F. H., & Co.—4 cs soap.
Schieffelin & Co.—17 pks wool fat.
American Motor Co.—1 pge candles.
Strohmeyer & Arpe—75 bls fish.
National City Bank of New York—11 bls rubber.
Kronfeld, Saunders & Co.—4 cs shells.
Richard, C. B.—1 cse films.
Corbett, M. J., & Co.—2 cs hat leather, &c.
Snow's Express Co.—2 cs woolens.
Van Ingen, E. H., & Co.—14 cs woolens.
Lippincott, J. & Co.—10 cs books.
Lazard Freres—1 bkx skins.
Aero Club of America—1 crte machinery, 1 cse printed matter.
Witcombe, McGeachin & Co.—386 rolls linoleum.
Wright & Graham Co.—427 cases tea.
Ullmann, J.—4 bls skins.
Arnold & Zeiss—134 cs rubber.
Brown Brothers & Co.—76 cs dragon's blood, 2 cs gum.
American Shipping Co.—3 cs books.
Adams Express Co.—96 cs books.
Leaker & Bernstein—117 cs sponges.
Oelrichs & Co.—29 cs pictures, &c.
Stechert, G. E. & Co.—12 pgs periodicals.
Milbank, Leaman & Co.—3 cs woolens.
Vandegrift, F. B., & Co.—1 champagne.

Bernard, Judae & Co.—10 bdls cheese.
American Express Co.—20 bdls cheese, 3 cs cognac.
Mouquin Wine Co.—1 cse liquor, 38 cs oil.
Kuauth, Nachod & Kuhne—107 cs mushrooms, 1 do pamphlets.
Lazard Freres—26 cs sardines, 8 do preserves.
Acker, Merrall & Condit—50 cs wine.
Dubois, Geo. F.—4 cske vermouth, 4 cs wine.
Heidelbach, Ickelheimer & Co.—11 cs shelled walnuts.
Brown Bros. & Co.—100 bls shelled walnuts.
First National Bank of Chicago—800 cs shelled walnuts.
Bischoff, H., & Co.—25 bgs rough wood.
Baumert, F. X., & Co.—50 bdls cheese.
Erie Despatch Co.—6 bdls cheese.
Galle, S., & Co.—50 bdls cheese.
Rathenberger & Co.—190 bdls cheese.
Haupt & Burgi—50 bdls cheese.
Sheldon & Co.—10 bdls cheese.
Percival, C.—50 bdls chee.
Stone, C. D., & Co.—30 bdls cheese.
Phoenix Cheese Co.—50 bdls cheese.
Petry, P. H., & Co.—10 bdls cheese.
Reynolds & Dronig—15 bls cheese.
Fougera, E.—41 cs filter paper.
Munroe, J., & Co.—22 cs mushrooms, 15 cs peas, 8 do beans, 10 do mixed vegetables, 24 do peas, 25 do olives, 12 bdls capers, 10 do fish, 20 do mdse.
Austin, Nichols & Co.—25 cs olive oil, 14 do mushrooms.
Order—14 cs factice, 13 do gum, 14 cake gum, 255 cakes tea, 3 do opium, 5 do window frames, 8 bls skins, 8 pgs. skins, 1 cse skins, 2 do horse hair, 2 do silk goods, 8 bls raw silk, 6 pgs hair nets, 200 pgs tea, 246 cs sardines, 30 rolls jute bagging, 1905 bags potatoes, 7 cs raw feathers, 10 do hatters' fur, 2 do tissue, 10 do rabbit hair, 31 pgs crude rubber, 7 cs vegetables, 5 do fish, 10 do syrups, 2 do liquors, 150 do shelled walnuts, 15 bdls cheese, 8 bls buchu, 2 cs grandfather's clocks, 2 do leather
Holders original bill of lading—19 bls opium, 15 cs calabashes, 5 bls buchu, 4 cs calabash bowls, 3 bls sheep skins, 2 cs ostrich feathers, 6 octs wine, 22 cs ostrich feathers, 4 do feathers, 8 bls skins, 28 bags argols, 3 bls sheep skins.

The cargo consisted of high-class freight, which had to be taken quickly on board and which could be just as quickly discharged. The articles were such as fine laces, ostrich feathers, wines, liquors, and fancy food commodities.

MORE BENEFITS PLANNED.

Many Stage Stars Volunteer for Cohan Theatre Concert To-night.

Additional benefits for the Titanic sufferers were announced yesterday. There will be a big concert at the George M. Cohan Theatre, Broadway and Forty-third Street, to-night. Samuel H. Harris will act as stage manager. Those who will appear include Blanche Ring, Henry Gilfoil, Wellington Cross, Lois Josephine, Clarence Oliver, and Florence Shirley of "The Wall Street Girl" company; George M. Cohan, Eddie Foy, and members of the "Over the River" chorus; Raymond Hitchcock and the pony ballet of "The Red Widow" company; Nat C. Goodwin, Frank Tinney, Brice and King, Harry Connor, Ethel Kelly, Charles J. Ross, and the Dolly twins, from the Moulin Rouge; Fanny Brice, Jean Schwartz, Anna Chandler, Al Plantadest, Fred Niblo, and Howard and Howard, from the Winter Garden; Tempest and Sunshine, Yvette, and others. The performance will begin at 8 o'clock promptly.

A $2 dinner for the benefit of the Titanic sufferers will be given at the Café Boulevard, Second Avenue and Tenth Street, on Tuesday evening, under the auspices of Charles H. Steinway, President of the Steinway Piano Company. Ruth St. Denis, Arthur Friedheim, and other artists have volunteered their services for the cabaret performance. The proceeds of the dinner will be distributed through the women's relief fund, of which Mrs. Nelson Henry is Chairman.

KEPT BAD NEWS SECRET.

Victorian's Passengers Not Told of Disaster Until They Landed.

HALIFAX, N. S., April 20.—Not one of the 1,424 passengers on board the Alan Line steamer Victorian knew of the Titanic disaster until they reached here to-day. The Victorian sailed from Liverpool April 12. The reason given by the officers for keeping back the information was the fear of causing uneasiness on board.

The news of the disaster was received by the Victorian eight hours after it occurred. The persons on board who knew of the message received were the wireless operator and Capt. Outram. This was received from the Carpathia, via the Baltic, on Monday, and the dispatch gave the number of lost and saved.

Capt. Outram said no bodies or wreckage were sighted, although a lookout was kept. He said he had to go very far south to avoid collision with icebergs. Thirteen large icebergs were passed at one time, and an apparently limitless stretch of heavy field ice.

LAURENTIC SEES NO BODIES.

Passes Over the Titanic's Course and Finds Nothing.

HALIFAX, N. S. April 20.—The White Star liner Laurentic, which arrives to-day from Liverpool, will bring no tidings to encourage hopes that any bodies of victims of the Titanic may be recovered.

In a wireless message early to-day Capt. Mathias of the Laurentic reported that he had kept a careful lookout while passing over the Grand Banks, and had seen neither bodies nor wreckage. The Laurentic came over practically the same course as the Titanic.

GOV. AND MRS. DIX SAIL.

Many Others on Lapland Had Been Booked for the Titanic.

The Red Star liner Lapland, for Antwerp via Dover, sailed yesterday, having among her passengers a number who had booked to sail on the Titanic, scheduled to sail from New York for Southampton at noon yesterday. Among these were Gov. and Mrs. John A. Dix.

J. Bruce Ismay, President of the International Mercantile Marine, had also expected to sail by the Lapland, but his departure was deferred because of the objections of the United States Senate investigating committee, which desired to further examine him regarding the wreck of the Titanic. John E. Mason, Gov. Dix's Secretary, had also booked by the Titanic, and he, too, was one of the Lapland's passengers.

There was a large number of friends at the pier to wish the Governor and Mrs. Dix a happy voyage. Just before the liner sailed Gov. Dix received the reporters.

"This is the first vacation I have had," said Gov. Dix, "since the campaign of 1910, and I feel that I need the rest. There is not a thing I care to say on politics. Neither is the Brandt case occupying any of my attention at the present time. Before leaving, however, I wish to renew my expressions of sympathy for the sufferers of the Titanic disaster and to commend as highly as words can the valor, courage, chivalry, and the splendid manhood of the men who sacrificed their lives on that dreadful occasion that women and children might be saved."

Among others sailing on the Lapland were Mr. and Mrs. Samuel Bell, Mr. and Mrs. James Fenimore Cooper, Mr. and Mrs. C. Temple Emmet, Baron Oscar Van Loo, Sir Donald Mann, Miss Alice Neilson, the opera singer; Baroness von Reiswitz, Mr. and Mrs. Oren Root, Simon Saks, Dr. J. Ford Thompson, Major E. Vincent, Dr. and Mrs. Ray P. Waldon, and Mrs. Edward F. Wyman.

Partial manifest of the *Titanic*

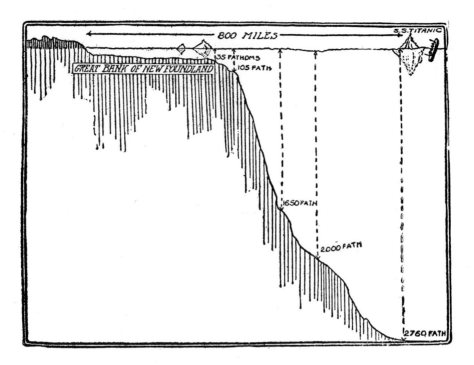

Depth of the ocean where the *Titanic* went down

The above etching shows a diagram of the ocean depths between the shore of Newfoundland (shown at the top to the left, by the heavily shaded part) to 800 miles out, where the *Titanic* struck an iceberg and sank. Over the Great Bank of Newfoundland the greatest depth is about 35 fathoms, or 210 feet. Then there is a sudden drop to 105 fathoms, or 630 feet, and then there is a falling away to 1650 fathoms or 9900 feet, then 2000 fathoms or 12,000 feet, and about where the *Titanic* sank 2760 fathoms, or 16,560 feet.

Crowds outside the White Star Line office in New York City seeking news of the *Titanic*

Lifeboats, as seen from the *Carpathia*

Survivors of the *Titanic* on board the *Carpathia*, taken after they were rescued

Note found in bottle washed ashore

Harold Bride, one of the two wireless operators on board the *Titanic*, being carried ashore from the *Carpathia*. One of the last men to leave the ship, Bride jumped into the sea and floated until rescued. Although suffering from frostbite, he helped the wireless operator of the *Carpathia* to send hundreds of wireless messages ashore.

J. Bruce Ismay, head of the White Star Line, before the Congressional Investigating Committee

"*It seems like trying to find a single star in the universe.*"

—Tom Paschall,
  deckhand on board the *Gyre*

CHAPTER III

THE TEST RUN

A number of us on board the *Gyre* were wishing we were ashore
on the second day out. Seasickness had struck. The cook, in an
attempt to prepare us for the rough seas ahead, had fed us rich,
fatty porkchops. The ploy had worked, not only on me but on
some scientists, crewmen, and other "excess baggage" as well.

Jack Grimm and Jim Drury were the most sympathetic to those
of us who were bedridden. Grimm went from bed to bed like a
mother hen, genuinely concerned. He said the *Gyre*'s radio had
already received eight calls from the media asking if anything was
happening. He also said a sailor had been swept overboard from a
ship fifty miles away and perished. A life preserver had been
thrown to him, but it landed too far away. Another sailor had
jumped into the water, held the man as long as he could, but lost
him before the ship could turn around. Very comforting to a sick
man, I can attest.

Drury's assistance was more practical. He brought seasick pills.

Everyone readily swallowed them except Mike Harris, a Christian Scientist. Harris suffered more and longer than anyone else.

Being confined to a bunk and being told to "just relax and roll with the motion of the ship" provided me with time to study the specific written search philosophies of Doctors Ryan and Spiess.

A number of considerations guided the search. The first and most obvious was to get us as close as possible to the place the *Titanic* went down. Starting at the beginning, Ryan and Spiess looked to the history books.

The *Titanic*'s distress position (CQD) of lat. 41°46'N and long. 50°14'W was telegraphed by the ocean liner's second radio operator Harold Bride shortly after midnight on April 15, 1912. The scientists assumed the location corresponded to a dead-reckoning calculation using the recorded heading and speed of the vessel since the evening's celestial fix, which was taken approximately five hours before striking the iceberg.

The fly in the ointment was that an error of one knot in determining the ship's velocity would have produced an error of five nautical miles in the CQD position. When Ryan, Spiess, and others compared the CQD position transmitted by the *Titanic* with the location of the ice floes reported by other ships in the general area that night and the following morning, they found that the *Titanic* gave a position well into or even west of the ice floe, rather than on its east edge where, in retrospect, she seems to have been.

The *Titanic* would not have stopped dead in the water after the collision. The impact of the glancing blow that tore the gash in the lower portion of the ship probably slowed her progress and caused her to veer off her course, but at a speed of twenty-three knots it is likely the *Titanic* continued for as much as two miles before stopping. It is not known precisely how the course of the ocean liner changed after striking the ice, but it was reported that the vessel did veer initially to the left (toward the south) to avoid a direct head-on impact with the iceberg when it was first sighted.

Every piece of evidence available was taken into account in the scientists' thinking about the *Titanic*. If the *Titanic* was close enough to have been visible from the *Californian*, as was reported after the sinking, then it was possible the *Titanic* changed to a northerly or southerly heading. Eyewitness accounts on the *Californian* relate seeing a large, well-lit vessel, which, while steaming westward on the southeastern horizon, suddenly changed to present a much smaller profile.

The scientists on board the *Gyre* also had a hypothesis that the CQD position was miscalculated or read incorrectly from the navigation charts, based on a discrepancy of twenty-three minutes. The hypothetical discrepancy was inferred by comparing the time that the second radio officer testified he sent the CQD position and the time it was logged in at Cape Race. The error was thought to have occurred from an oversight in accounting for retarding the ship's local time at the conclusion of the 2000 to 2400 watch and would have resulted in the *Titanic*'s CQD position being eight miles too far to the west.

Millions of dollars were being risked on the search, and the scientists had taken everything into account. They studied the *Californian*, which was hove to in an ice pack the night of April 14. Her latitude was well-determined with an evening celestial fix, and this plotted her eighteen miles north of the *Titanic*'s inferred track line. Officers of the *Californian* testified they saw a large ocean liner steam into the area, suddenly turn and move away, and later some of them reported seeing rockets in the sky. If that vessel had been the *Titanic*, concluded Spiess and Ryan, it was unlikely she was farther west than long. 50°10′ or farther south than lat. 40°40′. Based on the position of the *Californian* that night and the following morning, the rescue operation took place south of lat. 40°45′N and east of long. 50°10′W.

After the sun rose on the morning of April 15 the *Californian* was joined at the CQD position by the *Mount Temple*. The logs of the *Mount Temple* reported two separate celestial positions very close to each other that provided the scientists with a good longitudinal estimate for the westward limit of the ice floe. It was unlikely the floe extended, except in local patches, farther west than long. 50°13'W at lat. 40°42'N. The floe was estimated to have been between five and nine miles in width; thus, if the *Titanic* struck the iceberg shortly after entering the region of the floe (little ice was reported by the lookout prior to the collision), it was probable the event took place no farther west than lat. 50°08'N, and it was possible it occurred as far east as long. 50°03'W. "It is assumed by us," wrote the scientists, "that the*Titanic* slowed to a stop on a southerly heading parallel to the eastern edge of the ice floe."

The *Carpathia*, heroine of the disaster, was fifty-eight nautical miles southeast of the CQD position when she changed heading and put on full speed to come to assist the mortally distressed *Titanic*. When the *Carpathia* performed her gallant rescue work, there was no floating wreckage of the sunken ship to be seen.

The searchers aboard the *Gyre* assumed that the *Carpathia* was not very much north of lat. 40°45'N; otherwise, the lifeboats could not have been reached at the reported time because of the limited speed of the *Carpathia*. Furthermore, the *Carpathia* located the lifeboats at the eastern limit of the ice floe, and the floe had extended to the horizon in a northward direction. There was no fix made by the *Carpathia* when the rescue operation started, since considerable maneuvering was required to bring the lifeboats on board. A moderately increasing wind of six to twelve knots was blowing, but its direction was not known to the scientists. In any event there had been *no* wind blowing when the *Titanic* hit the iceberg, and none when she sank. Nor was the *Titanic* locked into the icepack, because the passengers in lifeboats described no difficulty moving away from the ship for distances up to a mile and more. One of the lifeboats rowed northward—toward the lights of a mystery vessel—without encountering dense ice.

The best possible oceanographic search team had been assembled, and its conclusions as to the location of the great ship were almost surely the most accurate ever formulated:

- The collision location was not farther westward than long. 50°15'W and more likely not farther westward than long. 50°10'W.
- The collision location was not farther eastward than long. 50°00'W.
- The collision latitude was not farther north than lat. 40°55'N, but could have been as far south as lat. 41°35'N.
- The *Titanic* drifted for 2.5 hours before sinking and could have covered a distance of 0 to 4 miles.
- After leaving the sea surface it is highly unlikely the *Titanic* traveled a horizontal distance greater than 2 miles.
- The *Titanic* remained at the eastern limit of the ice floe between collision and sinking.
- The lifeboats remained at the eastern limit of the ice floe between collision and sinking.
- The lifeboats remained at the eastern limit of the ice floe and drifted for 2 to 3 hours before being sighted by the *Carpathia*.
- The lifeboats could have drifted three miles from the sinking location before being sighted (they were spread out over an area of several miles).
- There is no way to estimate the exact direction and strength of the drift, but bodies were picked up 10 days later 50 miles directly east of the CQD.
- The *Carpathia* had no difficulty immediately finding the lifeboats using dead-reckoning navigation based on the previous evening's celestial fix.
- The ice floe had been reported in the shipping lanes for 6 days prior to the disaster, and at least two other vessels suffered damage from collisions; from their writings the floe appeared to have been traveling very slowly eastward and southward at under one knot (a few miles a day).

The scientists summarized there was a "high probability" the remains of the *Titanic* were in an area bounded on the north by lat. 41°55'N, to the south by lat. 41°35'N, to the west long. 50°20'W, and to the east by long. 49°55'W. The search area lay on the upper continental rise at the base of the continental slope southeast of Newfoundland. The water depths would range from 1,900 to 2,200 fathoms, and the area was bisected diagonally by a submarine canyon whose width ranged from 0.3 to 1.5 miles. The relief between the canyon floor and the canyon rim varied from 10 to 100 fathoms. It was here, in what the scientists had named Titanic Canyon, that we hoped to find the ship.

The first premise of our search was that we should be looking in this location, but in a way it would be like going to a childhood fishing hole but on a colossal scale. Our line was more than twenty thousand feet long, our lure weighed many times more than even Moby Dick. But now that I knew which was our fishing hole, I looked to our equipment.

Titanic Canyon had been surveyed originally by the U.S. Navy, using multibeam sound-echoing techniques. The survey established that the plateaus on either side were smooth, with gradients of only .001.

The 1981 expedition, besides finding and photographing the *Titanic*, and arranging for subsequent recovery operations, intended to go far beyond what the Navy had done. For example, two magnetic maps would be drawn. One would contour the total magnetic field intensity from near-bottom measurements. It would be crucial to determine if anomalies were sufficient in amplitude, distribution, and strength to correspond to a single Titanic-size magnetic source. The second map would be made from the sea surface relying on towed magnetometers.

The first map would prove by far the more valuable to our mission. In the map produced by sea surface–towed magnetometers, regional anomalies were greatly reduced in amplitude and local small anomalies were not apparent. It became clear that the magnetic signature of something even as large as the *Titanic* could not be picked up with a surface-towed sensor. Fortunately, the vehicle to be towed just off the bottom would be more than sufficient to detect even very small magnetic anomalies.

Two sonar systems would be employed. One was mid-range and would sonify the sea floor across a six-kilometer-wide swath. The sound pulses would be emitted every four seconds or once approximately every three meters as the towed vehicle advanced along the bottom. With this system it was possible to receive a pulse every second by reducing the range to 1.5 kilometers.

The mid-range sonar would be towed between fifty and two hundred meters above the sea floor and was equipped with a sub-bottom reflection profiler. In other words, if the *Titanic* was buried, we still might be able to "see" her. However, it turned out that because of the highly reverberant ocean floor surface somewhat peculiar to the search area, sub-bottom acoustic penetration was not always possible. The mid-range sonar output would be displayed in the *Gyre*'s laboratory on dry electro-sensitive paper.

The second type of sonar employed was a Deep Tow Instrumentation vehicle that sonified a 1.5 kilometer swath and emitted a sound pulse every two seconds. This was a higher-range frequency system with the ability to resolve smaller objects than the mid-range system could handle; this was important if the *Titanic* had broken up and lay in pieces. The Deep Tow Instrumentation vehicle was also equipped with a sub-bottom profiler whose data were displayed as a true-depth presentation using a high-resolution pressure sensor. Unlike the mid-range sonar, images were displayed on wet electro-sensitive paper.

Of course, these sophisticated methods—both for locating magnetic fields and objects, and employing sonar—had tremendous potential for government and private industry alike. Everyone realized that, particularly Jack Grimm and the scientists, but success in related pursuits was considered peripheral on this trip. Money—lots of it—and reputations—important ones—had been staked on finding the *Titanic*.

Because of the extensive search conducted in 1980 and the location of fourteen possible targets, the 1981 search operated on the assumption that the *Titanic* was more or less intact but acoustically obscured by nearby geological features. The scientists thus were concerned with getting the magnetometer readings the 1980 search had gone without and with shorter range side-looking sonar than had been employed the previous year.

Of course, it wasn't that simple. The sea is forever in motion, and there are no surface landmarks at sea. As a result, we had to use five acoustic transponder units spaced in locations five kilometers apart to optimize coverage of the suspected target areas and most of Titanic Canyon. Initial navigational positions were refined by a successive approximation process as multi-transponder fixes were accumulated during the search. We hoped these techniques would enable us to know where we were at all times with respect to the ocean floor, although the water on which we sailed was always moving.

This is not as easy as it might seem. Cameraman Jack Cosgrove, an expert deep sea diver, told how he once found a sunken galleon less than a mile off the shore of Tampa, Florida, in some two hundred feet of water. Cosgrove fixed its position with landmarks on the coastline but, despite returning dozens of times, was never able to locate the ship again. If a vessel a mile off the coast of Tampa in two hundred feet of water was nearly impossible to find again, it took no imagination to perceive the difficulties in relocating a ship in the Atlantic Ocean two and one half miles underwater. It would indeed be a tragedy if the *Titanic* were found and then lost again because of inadequate navigational equipment.

Two separate photographic systems would be used in the search. One met the following criteria:

- It had a high-capacity (several thousand frames) color still camera with electronic 250 watt-sec strobe for high-resolution photo documentation, but red color would only be seen when and if the camera could be maneuvered within less than 10 meters of the seabed.

- It had a color-TV capability, and a six-hour recording time was achieved by mounting a VHS cassette recorder in a hollow glass sphere, and in addition a 250 line resolution was attained with 500 watts of illumination.
- It had a black-and-white television capability with the signals displayed live on the *Gyre*.
- It could be lowered in a compact vehicle protected on all sides to reduce the possibility of fouling in the wreckage.

The vehicle that carried the second photographic system was equipped with four cameras:

- Two 35mm cameras forward with 150 feet of black-and-white film capacity (one of these was sometimes loaded with 100 feet of 200 ASA Ektachrome film, and approximately 40 square meters of sea floor were photographed in a single frame).
- One Stern 35mm camera with a wide-angle lens providing approximately 170 square meters of coverage.
- One Stern snapshot TV camera with telemetry to the *Gyre*.
- Also, one 250 watt-sec strobe dangled 8 meters beneath the vehicle.

On both photographic systems the cameras were pointed straight down, and the altitude was constantly monitored with the acoustic profiler. The strobe was fired from the surface when the cameras were at a correct height.

Another important tool of the scientists was the technology to record data in digital form as the search was taking place. A computer was used in real time to carry out navigational calculations, and a Hewlett-Packard desk-top computer processed and recorded location data. Newly built electronics and telemetry permitted more rapid input of information and allowed the computer to produce clearly discernible profiles of objects that in the past had simply been too small.

Fred Spiess's search philosophy was the product of more than four decades at sea and innumerable successes finding wrecks. As was the case when he looked to find the wreck's location, historical data was again Spiess's guide to understanding his prey. He had studied the U.S. Senate hearing into the *Titanic* disaster and the United Kingdom board of inquiry findings as well. He found the book *The Titanic and the Californian,* by Peter Padfield, particularly fascinating because it dealt with navigational material. Spiess also had encyclopedic knowledge not only of present-day navigational techniques but those in use in 1912. All of this, of course, was merely preliminary. Spiess was simply unaccustomed to failing, and the most careful planning was both desirable and incumbent.

Spiess knew from eyewitness reports of the tragedy that the *Titanic* was more or less in one piece when she went under. He was intimately familiar with other sinkings in which ships left the surface essentially intact and showed no damage following impact on the sea floor. "It seemed reasonable," Spiess wrote, "to expect *Titanic* to be more or less intact, and presenting a good sonar return, with good shadows, when viewed by side-looking sonar."

The scientists knew fairly well where the *Titanic* had to be, unless the ship's navigation was so poor that her SOS position was in error by more than ten miles. It seemed impossible, since that implied corresponding errors for other ships as well. More likely, problems would be encountered in other areas: the *Titanic* might lie in a geologically disturbed area such as a canyon, or slump scar, where the sonar could not separate the image of the ship from the surrounding irregular terrain. The ship might lie at right angles to the search track and, as a result of yawing the tow body, send back too few echoes to be recognized. The *Titanic* might have broken up on impact or been disturbed by turbidity currents, so she would not present the size sonar target necessary for recognition on a long-range scale (the danger here could include partial or complete burial) or a turbidity current landslide could have transported it out of the area completely or smeared her out to such an extent that she no longer existed as a definable entity. No one wanted to believe in these possibilities. The *Titanic* was whole; it had to be, or nearly so, and that was how she would be found. Some even believed, and there was scientific basis for it, that we would find supplies and bodies in an eerie state of suspended animation.

The magnetometer was expected to play a key role. The presence of a large amount of steel induces a local disturbance in the earth's field both from the magnetic susceptibility and from permanent magnetization acquired when the steel was forged and the ship was constructed, and the magnetometer would be used to measure the near-bottom total field intensity. The recognition problem was to tow the magnetometer close enough to the wreckage (two Titanic shiplengths) to detect a magnetic anomaly of either greater amplitude or more important shorter wavelength than would be produced by local and geological features.

Unfortunately, the search area was in a region of large anomalies produced principally by buried volcanic bedrock of the ocean crust. Another potential difficulty was the presence of glacial boulders carried to the area by floating icebergs, and these boulders from Greenland and Canada were metamorphic and igneous rocks with strong magnetic susceptibilities and permanent magnetization. A dense field of large boulders could present a local magnetic disturbance not dissimilar from the dispersed wreckage of a large ship that was broken up, scattered, and buried in a landslide.

A logistical problem was that once a target was initially recognized either by its magnetic disturbance or as a sonar image, the *Gyre* would long since have passed over the region of interest, since the towed vehicle might be up to two miles behind the ship.

At least six hours would be needed to bring the towed vehicle back into the area of promise for a second or third pass, usually at a different angle and distance, to learn more about the target characteristics. Once again, pinpoint navigation was of the essence.

The most important aspect of target confirmation depended on the photography and video recording equipment. The sonar and magnetometer, vital as they were, served as a means of directing our search—and therefore our camera systems—to the right areas. Obviously, what Grimm and his investors wanted was at least one picture of the wreck. And then he would be back at the earliest date with the *Aluminaut* to begin recovery operations.

Here there was a potential conflict between the desire for promotional publicity for the motion picture and the right of the media to news, and the need for secrecy if the *Titanic* were actually found. If exact coordinates were given as to her location, other parties probably would try to beat Grimm back to the site. But we couldn't worry about that until we had found her.

The night the *Titanic* had foundered there were no raging winds. The air was cold, but the sea was smooth, perhaps intensifying the seeming calm that prevailed on ship. Many people aboard believed the ship could not possibly sink, and if they stayed on board they could wait for the rescue ship. Others faced their fate as they were brought up to: bravely and unflinchingly, as good Victorians and Edwardians.

Eyewitness accounts report a number of acts of heroism that night. Mrs. Isidor Straus, standing hand in hand with her husband: "I will not leave him," she said. "We are old. We can best die together." Miss Elizabeth Evans gave up her seat on a lifeboat to Mrs. J. J. Brown: "Your need is greater than mine. You have children who need you, and I have none."

Rigel, a huge black Newfoundland dog, was a hero as surely as any human. Rigel belonged to the first officer, who perished with the ship; for three hours he swam in the icy water, saving a lifeboat of people from an almost certain death when the rescue ship

Carpathia almost rammed the small lifeboat when it drifted in the path of the ship. Unseen by the *Carpathia*, the lifeboat had gotten too close to the rescue vessel's starboard bow, and it seemed sure she would be rammed and sunk. Those in the lifeboat were too exhausted to cry out. At the last moment Rigel's barking attracted the attention of the *Carpathia*'s captain, and all, including Rigel, were saved.

Meanwhile, our night too was long, particularly when many of us were still feeling ill, and I waited in my bunk. Sleep was impossible and it was a good quiet time to continue with my research. I read a report written by Bill Ryan about the fourteen targets located in 1980.

Target Number One was situated in the thalweg (main navigable channel) of Titanic Canyon and represented by a distinct acoustic shadow. The shadow indicated a feature with a height in excess of eighty feet and a length of nine hundred feet. The feature appeared to be bent. Of the fourteen targets, this was considered one of the three most likely.

Target Number Two was northwest of Titanic Canyon, two miles west of *Titanic*'s distress position. It was a reflective strip seven hundred feet in length and one hundred fifty feet wide.

Target Number Three, a reflective patch twelve hundred feet long with no shadow, was north of Titanic Canyon and seven miles northwest of the distress position.

Target Number Four lay on a gullied slope north of Titanic Canyon. It consisted of an irregular patch with two small shadows indicative of objects twenty to thirty feet high and one hundred to three hundred feet long. If this were the *Titanic*, the great ship had been broken up.

Target Number Five, like Number One, was in the thalweg of Titanic Canyon and appeared to be a very reflective linear object about seven hundred feet in length.

Target Number Six rested on the northern wall of Titanic Canyon and had been sonicated on three separate runs. A clear shadow was cast on one of the runs, but not on the other two. This target was considered one of the three with top priority.

Target Number Seven occurred at the base of the south wall of Titanic Canyon and was a broad reflective patch measuring eight hundred by two hundred and fifty feet.

Target Number Eight was nicknamed the big banana because of its curled shape. It was a crescent some two thousand feet across, and within the crescent were three small reflective patches, each about one hundred feet long.

Target Number Nine was located east of Titanic Canyon. On the first trisect it appeared as a very thin and strongly reflective object about six hundred feet long. A second pass revealed it to be a broad patch of numerous low-lying small targets. If this were the *Titanic*, she had been crumbled into bits like a giant cookie.

Target Number Ten, the "little banana," was a curled slump feature containing three reflective objects that cast shadows along the wall of Titanic Canyon.

Target Number Eleven, located near the rescue position, was imaged from only one direction and consisted of several separate objects; the *Titanic* was in large pieces if this target was what we sought.

Target Number Twelve, also near the rescue position and also made up of separate objects, was close to several circular craters with diameters of fifty to a hundred feet.

Target Number Thirteen was the favorite of most of the scientists. Grimm called it odds-on. Situated at the top of the northern bank of Titanic Canyon midway between the corrected distress position and the estimated rescue position, it was a linear reflective object approximately nine hundred to a thousand feet in length that cast a clear, large shadow very similar in shape and size to the expected form of an intact *Titanic* hull.

Target Number Fourteen was an object located northeast of Titanic Canyon at a junction between the canyon and a tributary joining it from the north. It consisted of a strongly reflective patch about eight hundred feet in length and two hundred feet in width.

These, however, were not the only proposed targets. Don Armand thought that if we came up empty after investigating them we should look where the lifeboats were found, since they stayed fairly close to each other and didn't row far.

Grimm had a different idea, but it also made sense: he suggested going west on the latitude where bodies had been picked up. For many days after the *Titanic* had gone down, bodies were being recovered, and the terrible trail of carnage formed an almost straight line. By following it, Grimm reasoned, and thus following the tide as it had prevailed at the time, we would be led directly to the great ship, even if her last CQD had been incorrect.

The discrimination phase of the survey was expected to take less than sixty hours. As soon as an appropriate short-wave-length anomaly was detected, the target causing the anomaly would be reimaged with the sonar adjusted for the highest resolution scale. Two or three acoustic navigation beacons would then be deployed around the target using one-mile baselines. Next, several additional sonar runs would be made to fix the target precisely in the coordinate system and to image it from three to four different angles. Forty-eight hours would be required to deploy the beacons and resurvey the target.

Once the target had been precisely defined and its orientation and altitude determined, the photographic phase of the survey would begin. "Approximately eight to ten days of 'on-station' time," summarized Dr. Ryan, "should be sufficient to locate the wreckage and complete an extensive photographic coverage. One should attempt where possible to construct overlapping mosaics of certain sections of the ship."

My curiosity about the targets and coordinates having been ignited, a trip to the *Gyre*'s lab, the hub of operations, seemed in order the following morning. Alone in the lab was the Scripps

Institute's Dr. Carl Lowenstein, the epitome of the scientist who spends more time with machines than people. Lowenstein seemed never to smile, in his eyes perpetual worry. His niche was a chair and desk at the extreme rear of the lab, and no one— excepting possibly Spiess and Ryan—seemed to know what he did. "Only seven people in the world understand Lowenstein," Nik Petrik quipped, "and nobody understands those seven people." The Scripps scientists exhibited an extreme protectiveness toward Lowenstein. He was not to be made the butt of jokes about weird scientists who talked to machines.

All of the tools for monitoring the search effort were located in the lab, including the machines that kept track of the deep-tow sonar. Radar, of course, uses a radio signal to bounce a beam off an object of different density from its surroundings. But radio signals dissipate rapidly in water. Sonar, on the other hand, reaches out a certain distance in a certain time and, measuring the time the signal takes to return, paints a computerized acoustical image of the object.

Carl Lowenstein was in charge of all computer operations aboard the *Gyre*. He would store all the information we received and could retrieve it instantly if we needed to return to a spot where a specific object was recorded by the magnetometer, the sonar, or any of the cameras. Looking around the lab it was clear that this was a first-rate operation.

Leaving the lab, I went up on deck. The water off the bow was calm and blackish green; the sky was light blue with pale fluffy white clouds. The *Gyre* had stopped, and Don Armand was on the bridge. We had reached the HEBBLE site.

It came as a surprise to the few of us aboard who had joined on at the last moment to learn that before looking for the *Titanic* there would be another expedition called HEBBLE, High Energy Benthic Boundary Layer Experiment.

"Would you believe this?" said Bobby Blanco. "The purpose of HEBBLE is to find nothing."

It was true. The Office of Naval Research was sponsoring the experiment, and the first goal was to find an area of the ocean bottom where virtually nothing existed. This would simplify studying the seafloor and characterizing its details. Another aim of HEBBLE was to research deepwater currents and undersea storms, and again a barren ocean floor was ideal.

The first transponder for the HEBBLE project was being let out off the fantail. The transponder was brilliant orange so it could be easily seen in the water. It would sink to the bottom and stay anchored there until the scientists wanted it back. Then a device would be triggered from the *Gyre*'s lab that would burn the wire holding it firm, and the transponder would return to the surface. Jim Drury stopped to watch the transponder being released. Despite his seasickness, so far the journey had been pleasant for him. He had something good to say about everyone. Lowenstein was a "genius" and really a very pleasant person. Captain Armand was "witty" and "erudite about the sea"; the movie crew was "very professional"; Fred Spiess and Bill Ryan were "giants," and Jack Grimm was a "Renaissance man." "Even you are probably not bad," said Drury.

As HEBBLE was conducted each person on board was assigned duties. Some of us, including Jack Grimm, drew the tedious job of winch-watching, which required merely watching the "fish" cable to be sure it didn't break. Others drew more interesting jobs.

Nik Petrik turned out to have skill navigating by the transponders and was kept on the job by Farre on a permanent basis. Occasionally, however, he would get the *Gyre* lost, which would bring Lowenstein, clutching his head with his hands, rushing from his computers in the back of the lab. The conversation was completely predictable.

"Nik, this is not a difficult job."

It was a difficult job for anyone but Lowenstein.

"I won't take your abuse, Lowenstein."

"A child can do it."

"I'm a cameraman, Lowenstein. I take pictures. If you keep harassing me, I'll quit."

"It's important to know where we are. Look, I'll show you. . . ."

"Don't shout at me."

Lowenstein wouldn't shout at anyone.

"I just want to see the job done right. It's really quite easy and simple."

"That's it, Lowenstein. One more word and I quit. You can get someone else. I was hired to help make a movie, not to be harangued by you."

Petrik was master of this situation. Lowenstein, his fingers dancing over buttons, would locate where the *Gyre* was and return to the lab. Petrik would gripe about looking for nothing and talk about unionizing on board.

John Jain was in charge of the complicated equipment that recorded magnetometer readings. If the *Titanic* was found on his watch, it would be Jain who would have the first notice.

John Farre stood in front of a huge bathymetric map giving orders to his watch team and telling the person in charge on the bridge precise instructions where the *Gyre* should be sailing.

Once HEBBLE was underway, things calmed down for the nonscientists aboard. During one particularly quiet time I asked Jack Grimm his reasons for being interested in the project. He answered as a true romantic, speaking very quietly, as if he had thought it all out.

"A lot of people don't live very exciting lives. They dream of doing something great, but probably they never will. They don't have the chance. I do. I was lucky. Not all luck. I was good too. I made money.

"People from all over the country asked if they could come along on this search. I wish I could take everyone, but I can't. But people can share in what we're doing. Last year there were stories all over the world reporting our progress. The same will happen here. Everyone who wished they could do what we're doing can at least be a part of the adventure. It beats reading about muggings and wars."

"You might make a lot of money from this."

"I haven't made any yet. I won't turn it down, though. I keep telling you the point is it's a great adventure, people will imagine they're along. Movies are an escape. So is TV. This—finding a great ship—is the same sort of fantasy."

"You think it's a creative way to use money?"

"Sure. So is the Space Program."

"Takes people's minds off problems."

"More than that. Gives them something enjoyable to think about."

"Most rich men use money to get richer."

"I've got enough."

"You don't want more?"

"Sure I do. But the fattest steer is always the first to be slaughtered."

Grimm talked about his past. He grew up in Wagoner County, Oklahoma, the son of a small-town businessman. He was a Marine in World War II, wounded on Okinawa, decorated, and given a ninety percent disability by the government. He went on to graduate from the University of Oklahoma with a degree in geology. He married a fellow student, a striking blond named Jackie, and they spent their honeymoon looking for a gold mine and camping in the wilderness.

In 1949 Grimm went into the Oklahoma oil fields and shortly thereafter drilled his first oil well. It came up a winner. Then came twenty-five dry wells in succession, and it looked like his days as a young wildcatter were over. The alternative was working for a major oil company as a petroleum geologist, taking orders from someone else, a position that paid well but hardly appealed to his gambler's instinct and sense of individuality.

"The phone company cut off my service after the twenty-fifth dry well," says Grimm. "I decided to give it one more chance, drill one more well, and I've had phone service ever since."

Grimm has more than that. He now also has an interest in some four hundred other oil wells, plus gold and silver mines, real estate, and even a small herd of buffalo. Unlike many oil men, he has stayed put in Abilene, Texas, overseeing his empire, bumping over dusty, almost nonexistent roads, through pastures, personally running his growing business.

Regardless of the merits of Grimm's search for the *Titanic* concerning the pleasure it would vicariously provide others (and many were interested), the equipment the tycoon had paid for and given to Columbia University, could very well produce discoveries of lasting merit. Nets would be dragged along the ocean bottom, 2½ miles down, and many of the scientists believed that sea life not previously known to exist might be brought to the surface. In a literal sense there were a number of areas where science knew more about outer space than what lay beneath the earth's own oceans. It was why astronaut Alan Shepard was interested in diving on the *Titanic* site, which he called "another frontier."

The search for the *Titanic* was a happy—if rare—instance when academics and industry (if Grimm and his investors could be so classified) had, if not identical goals, aims that dovetailed. The boy and the businessman in Grimm wanted to find the lost ship; by obtaining the gear to find the *Titanic* and actually searching for her, the scientists could also forward their important studies of the ocean floor.

Many of the scientists were geologists, and the oil man could converse with them as an equal. He was particularly pleased that the Smithsonian Institution had asked him if he would donate artifacts of the *Titanic*, should any be recovered. He assured the Smithsonian that he would have even if he had not been asked.

As the monotonous HEBBLE test went on, the galley was the place to be for companionship; and lunch after a stint on the winch-watch was no different. Grimm was wondering out loud whether he should deliver a speech he had been asked to give at Harvard. Tony Boegeman professed sympathy for the winch-watchers: "The primary difference between prison and the winch-watch," he philosophized, "is the added risk of drowning."

Mike Harris talked about a note he had been given by a woman from Maine. The note had been found in a bottle washed up on a beach and found its way to Harris when the woman read about the search for the *Titanic*. It read as follows: "Our ship is lost. All hope of being saved is abandoned. Jack Steward. Ill-fated *Titanic*."

Bill Ryan discussed the difficulty we could expect to experience trying to film the *Titanic*. He compared it to dangling a camera from the top of the Empire State Building and trying to take a close-up picture of a manhole cover while the wind blew at forty miles per hour. "But that's not the best example," Ryan said. "The *Titanic* is ten times deeper than the Empire State Building is tall."

The people buried inside the *Titanic*, the scientists thought, might have been kept in a perfect state of preservation. The idea was macabre.

Time on the winch-watch went agonizingly slow. Another danger was that Farre, for all his efficiency, tended to forget anyone was on the winch-watch (of course, no one reminded him, because the individual might be given the assignment), and thus no relief appeared.

To a group assembled later in the galley, Ryan proudly announced that "we are working in fifteen thousand feet of water, and basically there is nothing on the bottom." It might have been more diplomatic to have mentioned just the first part, because this was deeper than the equipment would be asked to function during the *Titanic* expedition. Mentioning "nothing," which brought a tremor of joy only to the diehard scientists, was guaranteed to provoke negative reactions among others.

"This HEBBLE business is becoming *unendurable*," mumbled Grimm.

"At least the equipment is working. That's a good sign."

"Might not be," said Bobby Blanco.

"How can the equipment working not be a good sign?"

"It was *expected* to work. Why was all this money spent if it wasn't going to work? Of course it works! The question is, for how long? What if it gets damaged on this idiotic project? What if just natural wear and tear causes it to malfunction before we ever get to the *Titanic* targets?"

That Bobby was a pessimist no one would deny. Also, he often made sense.

Grimm heard what the Cuban said and a cloud passed across his face.

"Another thing," Bobby said. "This equipment was paid for to look for the *Titanic*. I'll grant you, it was given to Columbia University, but we maintained the right to use it for five years. Why should HEBBLE come first, and us second?"

"The scientists seem to know what they're doing. You really think there's much of a chance the equipment will be damaged?"

"Maybe not. They might just lose it."

Lose it?

"I don't trust these guys. Look what happened last year. The most important thing on the search vessel is the magnetometer, so what do they do? How many magnetometers did they bring? They brought *one*, and lost it before the search had barely begun. It's lying on the floor of the ocean, like the *Titanic*."

"Why didn't they carry a back-up?"

"Who knows? Who knows why they're looking for nothing? But we did pretty good last year—look at all the targets we found—and probably would have found her for sure if we'd had a magnetometer along for the whole trip."

In the lab people were abuzz over the fact that an improvement devised by Carl Lowenstein for the side-scan sonar seemed to be working. We could now not only measure depth directly under-neath us but also off to the side. This was the first time such information had ever been recorded by a computer. Earlier pre-dictions that even if the *Titanic* were not found other important breakthroughs would result seemed to be coming true.

"Grimm," said John Jain, "might become famous for reasons he never intended."

"I don't think he would want to hear that."

"I'm *sure* he wouldn't."

Later, Ryan was asked what the chances were of finding the *Titanic* on this year's expedition. "I'd say fifty-fifty," he answered. "It would be one hundred percent sure if we had a hundred days to look."

This answer was related to Grimm. "Well," he said, "we don't have a hundred days. Croesus couldn't afford a hundred days, even if the weather permitted, which it wouldn't. The time we have is going to *have* to be enough."

Everyone had settled into a routine that wouldn't vary until we got down to the serious business of searching for the *Titanic*. Bobby Blanco had begun fishing for sharks with a homemade line baited with meat Eddie Vos was going to throw overboard (Bobby never caught anything, but the line was snapped, presumably by sharks, several times). Jack Cosgrove grew mellow about having to work long hours at no pay looking for nothing. Jack Grimm tried to persuade people to join his nightly gambling sessions: "I feel it in my bones, boys, my luck is about to change." Nik Petrik argued with whomever was nearby about which movie would be shown in the evening (these were fruitless debates, since Captain Armand owned the film tapes, and usually ended up deciding). And the scientists doggedly went on about HEBBLE, wrestling with heavy equipment, coaxing precise information out of delicate gear, generally working long, exhausting hours amid sneers and scornful glances from their "artistic" shipmates.

On July 5 the scientists decided to bring up the "fish," one ton of metal that appeared sturdy but carried the most sensitive devices. It had been towed at depths down to fifteen thousand feet, and now the scientists wanted to check her out. It was dangerous work, bringing this monster up, especially if the sea were rough, and it was getting that way. The "fish," dangling from the crane, might swing wildly out of control and pulverize some-one, or simply bash him thirty feet in the air and fifty feet out to sea.

The scientists had to have gone through the drill a thousand times. A poorly timed move, and hundreds of thousands of dollars of equipment could be gone, and maybe a few lives. Watching the military precision of their maneuvers, the *physical* strength it was clear they soon would have to exert to wrestle the fish aboard the *Gyre* while half hanging over the deck, it seemed construction workers or oilfield roughnecks would be better suited for this type of job. This contest was going to be strength against strength.

The scientists were spread all across the fantail, awash with water from the gathering waves. Spiess was in the middle of all of it, a frail, erect symphony conductor moving his people with precise, martinet hand movements.

"He shouldn't be out there. He's an old man and it's too dangerous," someone commented.

"It would be dangerous if *you* were out there," said Drury. "Just watch and enjoy it. You're seeing the best in the world."

A gray wave on this gray morning reached over the deck like a giant hand and slapped Spiess hard. He disappeared from view for a moment, inundated, but he emerged, still standing straight.

The muscle people—Farre, Wardlow, Jain, Chayes, Olsson— were on the starboard side, wearing bright-orange life jackets, hanging on to the railing, preparing themselves to overpower the one ton fish when it came boiling out of the depths.

Skip Gleason's job was the most important. That first night aboard the *Gyre* John Jain had said Gleason loved to take chances, and out on the fantail was proof of the remark. It would be very easy for Gleason to kill a number of people, or himself, if just for an instant he lost control of the fish. It could happen, and Gleason might not even be negligent. The waves were growing in height, size, and force, and they could decide that this California beach boy was insignificant and sweep him aside.

The movie crew was out in force; it was the first chance to show their wares. Petrik was aiming an expensive camera; Bobby Blanco was shooting from another angle; veteran Jack Cosgrove had his camera right up against Spiess. The authoritarian ocean-ographer could not be expected to react sympathetically to this invasion of his territory, but his demeanor at first seemed all out of proportion to the offense. He waved his arms, crazily and vio-lently, and although his words could not be heard over the crash of water, it was plain enough what he was screaming. He wanted Cosgrove out, right away, go! Cosgrove was not wearing a life jacket, and Spiess was trying to save his life. The "fish" was coming up, so were the waves, and a person knocked overboard had a quarter of a chance with a life jacket.

Mike Harris was on the fantail, directing. This was a dramatic scene, and the artist in him came through. He looked like a movie director, marshalling his troops; put Bobby here, Petrik there, humor Spiess, Cosgrove, put on a life jacket and get back out.

Lamont photographer Anita Brosius was on the fantail, furi-ously recording activities. There was a synchronization between her and the male photographers, easy to see but hard to identify.

Even Jack Grimm, out of bed earlier than usual, was on hand to observe. He was stepping gingerly, not a hint of false Texas bravado. But that was *his* "fish" coming out of the water; if it were lost he could forget his dream of finding the *Titanic*.

It happened without warning. The "fish" bubbled out of the water, glistening yellow, having been where no human had gone. It hung stark still over the water, five feet from the deck, not even a wobble, so surely did Gleason hold it. Skip inched it closer, not a trace of extra motion, remarkable because the ship rolled and waves banged the deck like artillery fire.

For a moment John Jain was going overboard. He was, it appeared, hanging from the railing by his ankles. Crash! Another wave came, and then Wardlow and Farre and the others had their arms around the torpedo and were wrestling and cradling it onto the deck.

Grimm was in the galley, relieved that his equipment was intact. For some reason he wanted to talk about his ancestors, most particularly one Ernest Washington Grimm, who had been Robert E. Lee's flag bearer. "Wounded seven times," Grimm said. "One time when he was shot Lee saved his life by running a silk handkerchief through the wound and pulling out the bullet."

Anita Brosius—her photographs of the fish rescue turned out to be best of all—was flushed with the success everyone felt. The fish had functioned beautifully on HEBBLE, and she was intrigued by "colonies of new sea life" we might find on the *Titanic*.

Now, with the HEBBLE tests complete, we could go in search of history.

"*All Saved From* Titanic *After Collision.*"

—headline in the
New York Sun
April 15, 1912

CHAPTER IV

THE TELLING
OF A GREAT
TALE

To those of us for whom the *Titanic* is simply an enormous ship that has always been sitting on the Atlantic's floor, it is difficult to imagine the response experienced by those who heard of its sinking immediately after it happened. Its foundering was one of those extraordinary events that occur only a few times in a lifetime: a profound moment that, even for those not even indirectly involved, had a palpably emotional impact. More than a horrible accident that resulted in the death of over fifteen hundred men, women, and children; it was a tragedy that saw innocents—guilty of nothing more than being possessed of the need or desire to cross the Atlantic Ocean—die needlessly.

If the passengers and crew on the *Titanic* itself were slow to realize what was happening, the world around them was slower still. To anyone walking the tilting deck of the *Titanic* and watching the loading of the lifeboats, the gravity of the situation was obvious. Elsewhere, as miscellaneous bits of news filtered in, it hardly seemed credible.

The first means by which word of the accident traveled was the wireless. The Marconi shacks of ships in the North Atlantic were the first to receive the coded plea for help at 12:15 A.M., *Titanic* time. The North German Lloyd steamer *Frankfurt*, the Allan liner *Virginian*, and others heard the call.

The Cunard liner *Carpathia* was not the first to respond—her wireless operator had been away from his post when the first distress signals came through—but the *Carpathia*'s response was the most important since she was the closest ship to reply.

"Come at once," the *Carpathia* was told. "We have struck a berg."

Radio communication in 1912 was not to be taken for granted. Messages had to be tapped out in a laborious translation of words to the letter-by-letter code. There were no satellites off of which to bounce the signals, so any message that had to travel a considerable distance had to be relayed—perhaps two or more times—or sent via a cable buried deep beneath the sea. At the best of times the air was likely to be abuzz with radio traffic, and the cables overloaded. When the news of the *Titanic*'s accident was transmitted, it was no exception.

A radio operator at Cape Race, Newfoundland, was the first landlubber to hear of the *Titanic*'s predicament. The *Titanic* only shortly before had been sending personal marconigrams from passengers and crew to the shore, which, in turn, would be relayed to their destination in New York or elewhere. The operator at Cape Race heard the bad news at the same time the other ships did.

The *Titanic*'s two wireless operators continued to send messages to the ships nearby, urging them to hurry to the rescue. On the *Carpathia* the messages were increasingly gloomy. "Come as quickly as possible, old man; engine room filling to the boilers."

On the other ships, the messages from the *Titanic* stopped abruptly, only slightly more than an hour after the first distress call had gone out. The *Titanic*'s radio broadcast range shrank as the ship lost power. She was isolated and for the next few hours, her fate was a secret.

In the United States on Monday April 15 an oblivious public woke up to its morning papers. The *Titanic* was already resting on the ocean floor. *The New York Times*, even then possessed of a penchant for accuracy, reported in its front-page headline, "NEW LINER TITANIC HITS AN ICEBERG: SINKING BY THE BOW AT MIDNIGHT: WOMEN PUT OFF IN LIFEBOATS."

As is so often the case in running a business where deadlines are omnipresent, the *Times* managing editor, Carr Van Anda, had been faced with the need to make an educated guess. His information was incomplete as the moment to go to press approached. He had received an Associated Press bulletin saying the ship had struck an iceberg. While calls to correspondents in Halifax and Montreal had confirmed the collision, little other news had been offered.

One fact—actually the absence of fact—led Van Anda to make a judgment. He decided that the lack of further word from the *Titanic* suggested the worst. His stories were careful and scrupulously accurate. But the impression left was that the ship had gone down.

A shocked public awaited more news, but no words were heard until the morning gave way to afternoon. We know now how wrong the next reports were, but on that Monday noon people wanted to believe them. In the North Atlantic a question had been delivered by a toneless electrical device incapable of raising its voice at the end of a sentence. "Are all *Titanic* passengers safe?" Another marconigram that began as a long paragraph had been truncated. One sentence of it, "Towing oil tank to Halifax," was picked up and combined with the first message. The result was wonderful news and quickly broadcast. "All *Titanic* passenges are safe. Towing to Halifax."

To a distant receiver the signal was barely audible. The operator, probably a novice playing with a new toy then entirely unregulated by the government, passed on a message so far from the truth as to be, in retrospect, tragi-comical.

The good news arrived by wireless and was presumed to be from the *Olympic*, relayed via Cape Race and Montreal to New York. Readers of the afternoon papers had reason to relax. The *Evening Sun* in New York ran a banner headline that read, "ALL SAVED FROM TITANIC AFTER COLLISION." In London, where word was heard from the United States via Atlantic cable, the population went to bed more than a few utterances of relief later, confident of the fate of the *Titanic*'s passengers. Little did they know what the morning would bring.

At the same time as the *Sun* hit the streets, David Sarnoff was atop Wanamaker's New York department store operating a wireless. Wanamaker's had a promotional gimmick to take advantage of the public's curiosity about the wireless. Operators were situated in Wanamaker stores, and the public was given a close look at the workings of the new-fangled system. It succeeded in drawing hundreds of customers.

It also may have provided David Sarnoff's career with just the impetus it needed to launch his ascending to eventual chairmanship of RCA. It was 4:35 P.M. when he received the message that delivered not only Sarnoff but also the wireless onto the front pages. The powerful wireless on the *Olympic*, sister ship of the *Titanic*, still 1,400 miles out to sea, relayed the message from the *Carpathia*, which had by this time picked up the survivors. The *Titanic* had foundered. Only 675 people had survived. The *Carpathia* was bound for New York.

At 6:27 P.M. a similar message from the captain of the *Olympic* reached the White Star Line offices. Moments later, Philip A. S.

Franklin, vice president of the International Mercantile Marine Company, acknowledged the sinking.

Franklin had staunchly maintained all day that the ship was unsinkable. A stout man, possessed of the assured demeanor appropriate to a man of his prominence, he had done his best to assure everyone that surely there had been some mistake. As he said later, "It never entered our minds that there was such a serious loss of life until six twenty-seven, when we got Captain Haddock's [of the *Olympic*] message." Positive thinking allowed Franklin to maintain that other ships might have picked up other survivors. By midnight, he was in tears. "I thought her unsinkable," he cried. "I do not understand it."

By Tuesday morning the word was well-known. *The New York Times* led with a full banner headline: "TITANIC SINKS FOUR HOURS AFTER HITTING ICEBERG." The time elapsed was wrong (two and one half hours was more like it), and the number of survivors was a bit high (the *Times* cited 866 survivors, the actual count was 713), but for virtually all of the first dozen pages of the Tuesday, April 16, 1912, edition, the *Titanic* and its passengers were the sole subject.

Names poured in from the Marconi service, from the *Olympic* to Cape Race, and to the wires of the Associated Press. Beginning at 5:30 A.M., bulletins were posted conspicuously in hotels, clubs, public buildings, and large stores. Handprinted in large dense type, the bulletins were lists of the survivors. Throughout the day a total of five lists were posted, the last of them at 6:30 P.M. Only four hundred names appeared.

It was the 9:00 A.M. bulletin that had the greatest impact. Coming as it did when thousands of workers were bound for their offices, perhaps fifty thousand people stopped for a look at the lists of one hundred seventy-six names. Thousands milled about the places where the names were posted, awaiting news of friends or relatives, or perhaps just curious about the brouhaha surrounding the mind-boggling event. Even for those disappointed at not finding a name among the four hundred, hope remained. There were said to be eight hundred or more survivors.

As word of the tragedy reached people, the first response was almost invariably shock. People who lost relatives or friends felt the acute sense of personal loss that only the coupling of freak chance and death can bring. Millions of others were affected by a morbid fascination. To many people, however, there was a sense of violation, a perception that something was wrong—badly, improperly, terribly wrong. Perhaps the resultant rage manifested by so many is akin to the anger Elisabeth Kubler-Ross has pointed out as one of the early reactions of a patient after being told his illness is fatal.

There was an immediate outrage at what seemed to many to be the lies they had been told about the survival of all the passengers. At the White Star Line offices on Tuesday morning, the crowds were so unruly as to require a growing number of policemen, first two mounted police, then six armed regulars, and more as the day wore on. The Lloyd's office in New York was similarly mobbed, as was the Cunard Line office, since it was the Cunard Line's *Carpathia* that was bringing the survivors to New York.

As if to feed the frustration, Tuesday and Wednesday were moments suspended in time. The *Titanic* had sunk, and everyone knew it, but people also wanted to know why and how. Those able to tell the tale were still at sea and not due to dock until Thursday. There was a steady flow of names of survivors, but the wireless was simply not sufficient to provide the vivid narrative, full of tales of cowardice and courage, that the world craved. To make matters worse, even when the names had all been sent, no further details followed. A radio silence had been imposed.

There was an immense appetite but a serious lack of hard information. Since the passenger lists were available, the papers offered thousands of words about John Jacob Astor and Archie Butt and the other notables who had been on board the *Titanic*, and devoted great spaces to the response of Theodore Roosevelt and others to the loss of the *Titanic* and its fifteen hundred passengers. But that was simply a smoke screen, mere filler while everyone waited for the survivors to dock and tell their stories.

In addition to profiles of the notables on board the newspapers found another means to try and sate the public's appetite. There were "experts" to question, and speculations to peruse. One of the first to be interviewed was the recently retired Chief Designer at Harland & Wolff.

Alexander Carlisle was the first to publicly air the matter of the lifeboats—that there was an insufficient number for the passengers on the *Titanic*. "The laws regarding ten-thousand-ton boats as the maximum is very old," he pointed out. The *Titanic* at forty-six-thousand-ton displacement had more than the requisite number of lifeboats (the statutes of the British Board of Trade required that any vessel displacing more than fifteen thousand tons had to have no less than sixteen boats; the *Titanic* had twenty). But the *Titanic* had been more than three times the size of the ships for which the statute was written. He speculated on aspects of the ship's design—the value of water-tight doors, for example—but it was the paucity of lifeboats that horrified people the most. And for good reason: the lack of lifeboats is still regarded as the single most important factor in the loss of life.

Also on that Tuesday, one Captain Inman Sealby, a veteran of twenty-five years of sailing the Atlantic, offered his theory on why the collision with the iceberg had caused the ship to sink. He was something of an expert on shipwrecks, having been in charge of the White Star liner *Republic* when she had sunk three years earlier after a collision with another ship.

"I believe," said Sealby, "that the *Titanic* struck an iceberg and glanced off, but that a portion of it under water, which could not be guarded against, struck her from the bottom and stove a great hole in her." On the following day, Wednesday, the papers featured the words of other experts—Hugo P. Frear, designer of the battleship *Oregon,* and Vernon H. Brown, retired general manager of Cunard, who supported Sealby's contention. It was not a head-on collision; they agreed. "The sides of a vessel are most difficult to protect," said Frear. "They are the most vulnerable spots in a steamship's anatomy, and it is my opinion that the *Titanic* struck the iceberg at an angle."

The absence of hard facts from the *Carpathia* had given such speculation space on the front pages. And the experts had come through. Their suppositions were remarkably accurate.

On Thursday, April 18, the *Carpathia* finally steamed into New York harbor. To the impatient thousands who lined the piers on Manhattan's West Side, the progress of the *Carpathia* up the Hudson was painfully slow. Relatives, friends, thousands of the curious, and virtually every reporter in town waited. At 9:35 P.M. the ship docked, and the gangplanks were affixed. The passengers walked off the ship, more than a little awed by their reception. A crowd of more than thirty thousand stood staring. A Salvation Army band played. Cries of joy and anguish were heard as loved ones were recognized or not to be seen.

The world finally got what they wanted as the passengers offered up their stories. The tales were a varied lot, some patently untrue, as was obvious to even the most credulous readers. There were contradictions galore (Captain E. J. Smith, for example, was last seen in an impossible number of places, both performing acts of great courage—according to one account, saving a child from drowning—and committing suicide). But as the survivors who chose to spoke to reporters, the public learned of the events that followed the iceberg's tearing the *Titanic*'s hull.

As had come to be the norm in the coverage of the *Titanic*, the *Times* had the most accurate coverage the following morning. The key article was Harold Bride's story. The second wireless operator aboard (his superior, Jack Phillips, perished) sold his story exclusively to the *Times* for one thousand dollars. It adorned five columns of the paper's front page that Friday.

His was a precise account of the activity in the *Titanic*'s Marconi shack, which, located adjacent to the bridge, had been at the center of activity. Starting with the first distress call, he led his readers through the hours before, during, and after the ship slipped beneath the sea. Bride himself was in the water, only one hundred fifty feet from the vertical hulk, when she disappeared.

"When at last the waves washed over the rudder there wasn't the least bit of suction I could feel," he concluded.

In the days that followed, the press reports were dominated by the stories of the survivors. As if the inherent interest in the tragedy did not provide sufficient justification for pouring barrels of printer's ink into the *Titanic* tale, the U.S. and British governments provided twin frameworks on which to hang weeks and weeks of news stories: the U.S. Senate and the British Board of Trade both launched investigations into the tragedy, first in New York, then in London.

Rarely has any event so dominated the front pages. The public's hunger for details was offered enormous dollops of personal tragedy, mixed with healthy portions of institutional ineptitude. One by one survivors, passengers and crew alike, took the stand, before the U.S. Senate, then before Britain's Board of Trade. Pitiful revelations were made of half-empty lifeboats being lowered, while hundreds remained behind on the sinking ship. Heroic stories were told of the men who had resigned themselves to their fate, who helped others to escape the flooding decks.

Most stories were told willingly, though J. Bruce Ismay found himself playing the roles of both scapegoat and hostile witness. He was asked hard questions. More than a few people felt he should have gone down with the ship, just as his subordinate Captain Smith had. Ismay's behavior came under even more intense scrutiny since he had had the bad faith to wire to shore from the *Carpathia* that another of the White Star Line's ships should be held a day so that he could return to England on it. His early exit was prevented, but it only made his visits to the witness stand all the more unpleasant.

J. Bruce Ismay had been a central figure in the drama. He was Managing Director of the White Star Line, and most observers found it incredible that Captain E. J. Smith, with a long and honorable record at sea, would recklessly have ploughed through iceberg-laden waters, particularly since it was to be his last voyage in charge of a ship. It had to be, these observers contended, that he was following orders from Ismay, who wanted to set a transatlantic speed record.

And who was in charge, if not Ismay? That too few lifeboats were aboard was tragically obvious. The *Titanic* had a swimming pool, private promenades, a gymnasium, luxurious restaurants, elegant saloons, gambling rooms and elevators, but too few lifeboats, as the chief senatorial inquisitor never tired of pointing out.

When the lifeboat Ismay was in was pulled aboard the *Carpathia* his first words were to a steward, "Hurry, for God's sake, and get me something to eat, I'm starved. I don't care what it costs or what it is. Bring it to me."

The steward, testifying at the Senate hearing, said Ismay handed him two dollars.

"Your money is no good on this ship," the steward claimed he told Ismay.

People around the world were shocked that Ismay had survived at all. It was felt he should have met the fate so willingly accepted by Captain Smith. Instead he found his way aboard a lifeboat packed with women and children.

At the Senate hearing, Ismay laid full responsibility for the sinking on Captain Smith. Even that august body would not buy this version.

That the Senate investigation was as thorough as it turned out to be was because so many prominent people perished aboard the *Titanic*. These victims had influential friends and relatives, and even the power of J. P. Morgan could not silence them. Archibald

Butt, military aide to President Taft, went down on the *Titanic*. Benjamin Guggenheim, copper magnate, was head of a family with reputed wealth of ninety-five million. George B. Widener, Philadelphia financier, socialite, and horse connoisseur had an estimated wealth of five million. And John Jacob Astor, the richest person on the *Titanic*, controlled one hundred and fifty million in real estate holdings.

Other notables who died aboard the *Titanic* were Jacques Futrelle, popular novelist and contributor to *Saturday Evening Post;* theater manager Henry B. Harris, who managed stars such as Peter Dailey, Amelia Bingham, May Irwin, and Lillie Langtry; railroad tycoon Charles M. Hays; Francis David Millet, Civil War hero, translator of Tolstoy, one of America's finest painters; William T. Stead, editor of *Review of Reviews,* peace activist, one of the best known journalists in the world; and Washington Augustus Roebling, who built the Brooklyn Bridge.

Ismay alienated observers with the smile he wore on his face during the Senate hearings. But more than his countenance, it was his efforts to clear himself by placing all blame on Captain Smith that were not received kindly. Smith's background was simply too impressive. He first went to sea as a young boy in 1869 aboard the *Senator Weber* and served seven years as an apprentice. Next he caught on with the *Lizzie Fennell*, a square rigger, as fourth officer, then the *Celtic* of the White Star Line, learning every duty a seaman needs to know, until in 1887 he became the *Celtic*'s captain. He also commanded the *Cufic, Runic, Brittanic, Coptic, Majestic, Baltic, Germanic,* and *Olympic*. Smith's was an extraordinary, almost unparalleled career, and it seemed ludicrous that on this occasion he would jeopardize a lifetime of accomplishment.

More ominous, the Senate investigation revealed, was that, unknown to the passengers, the *Titanic* was on fire. "The fire started in bunker Number Six," testified John Dilley, who spent all of his waking hours fighting it. "There were hundreds of tons of coal stored there. The coal on top of the bunker was wet, as all the coal should have been, but down at the bottom of the bunker the coal had been permitted to get dry. The dry coal at the bottom of the pile took fire and smoldered for days. The wet coal on top kept the flames from coming through, but down in the bottom of the bunkers the flames were raging."

The fire never was put out, the passengers were never informed. It was still being fought when the killer iceberg rendered the effort meaningless.

Both Captain E. J. Smith and J. Bruce Ismay were aware of the fire, had two opportunities to terminate the voyage, but chose to go ahead to their destinies (the one, down with his ship, the other, subject to monumental public denunciation, forced to live out his life in virtual seclusion).

Captain James Parton, Manager of the White Star Line, provided testimony to the Senate subcommittee that might have been directed to the *Gyre* and all those aboard. "Sinking in mid-ocean," said Captain Parton, "at the depth which prevails where the accident occurred, absolutely precludes any hopes of salvage."

Perhaps the high point in the investigation process was the revelation, first by a lowly seaman, that as the *Titanic* had gradually sunk into the sub-zero Atlantic Ocean, another ship, the *Californian*, was visible only a few miles away. Its wireless shut down for the night, its engines stopped because of the dangers of the icefield, its captain gone to his bunk, the *Californian* had waited patiently for sunrise. Its officers on watch had seen the rockets the *Titanic* sent up, and even sent word of them to the captain.

Captain Lord of the *Californian* was quoted in the press as saying, "I only wish I had known the *Titanic* was in danger. I would have been glad of the opportunity to go to her assistance just as fast as I possibly could," but few took him at his word. As a result of the incident, he lost his command with the Leyland Line. The public finally had their scapegoat.

On the other hand, they had their heroes as well. One of the brightest of them was Second Officer Charles H. Lightoller, the *Titanic*'s highest ranking survivor. He took the stand with the dignity of a man who had done his duty to the end. And he had. He hadn't climbed aboard a lifeboat but had gone down with his ship. He had got lucky and, at the last moment, had been ejected from the wreckage by a blast of air escaping from one of the great funnels. He had found an overturned, empty lifeboat to which to cling, along with some other freezing survivors.

His testimony was probably more crucial to the findings of both investigations than anyone else's or than any bits of evidence. And so simple, as well. He defended the honor of his fellow officers and of the White Star Line. His own heroic behavior added credence to his testimony, as he summed it up in his memoirs twenty-five years later, that the *Titanic*'s chance meeting with the iceberg was just that, a case of simple accident. "The disaster was just due to a combination of circumstances," he said, "circumstances that never occurred before and can never occur again. That may sound like a sweeping statement, yet it is a fact."

As April gave way to May and June 1912 the reporters focussed their energies on the two investigations. But their editors back in the newsrooms looked to vary the fare. The occasional oddity helped a bit, like the fainting of Harland & Wolff's Alexander Carlisle at a memorial service for the *Titanic* dead in St. Paul's Cathedral in London. Sermons read from pulpits all around the world filled more than a few "graphs," as well, as the greed of the White Star Line and the collective guilt of the wealthier classes in their endless quest for luxury garnered considerable clerical attention.

As always, however, the popular imagination was caught most

effectively neither by the hard news nor by the men of God and their railing at fate and sin; the "little" people had the greatest appeal. One who took advantage of an opportunity for fame and fortune in print that he otherwise would never have had and would never have again was a survivor named Lawrence Beesley. He offered his story to the newspapers not once, but twice. Barely two days after the *Carpathia* had returned the survivors to shore, Beesley summed up his opinions of the tragedy for *The London Times*. A week later, he elaborated on his original story in *The New York Times* at the request of Carr Van Anda.

As a schoolmaster, he did himself proud. The second and more detailed article was a pedagogical recitation. An acute observer, he both told his story and analyzed what he had seen. His essay had all the formal rigor of a lesson in rhetoric, yet also the controlled anger of a man who had seen a ship sink before his eyes and nearly beneath his feet.

Among the possible explanations for the wreck, the ever rational Beesley cited the sheer size of the *Titanic*. He dusted off the law of physics that says momentum is equal to the mass of an object times its velocity. "I wonder how it would be to display on the bridge of every ship [that formula]?" he pondered. To him the presence of the simple formula seemed a possible deterrent to steaming at foolhardy speeds in the ice zones.

Explanation aside, the *fault* was systematic; he asserted. It was an institutional guilt, and it extended to the governments—specifically the French, the American, and the British—that were charged with regulating the ships that traveled the high seas.

Beesley also saw a higher personal meaning. He admitted that for six years he had been a Christian Scientist, and that he had been traveling to America in order to "study the greater work in New York, Boston, and the west." He stated that it was his faith that had allowed him to retire to his cabin and accept his imminent death. Only after his acceptance of his fate, had he gone up on deck and, when an opportunity arose, taken advantage of it.

The New York Times, in an editorial response to Beesley's articles, commented only briefly on the sensibleness of the letter, then devoted itself to the subject of Beesley's religion. The editorial concluded, "Perhaps it would not be quite fair to ask Mr. Beesley why, with his fear so nearly eliminated, he did not remain in his cabin instead of going where he, and not another, would be invited into a boat, but the temptation to do so is strong."

Other and better-known names were to be seen by-lining newspaper pieces on the subject of the *Titanic*. George Bernard Shaw professed a "profound disgust, almost of national dishonor" on the pages of *The London Daily News*. "Why is it," he asked, "that the effect of a sensational catastrophe on a modern nation is to cast [it] into transports not of weeping but of an explosion of outrageous, romantic lying?" His criticism was of the oft-heard praises to be said about Captain Smith (said Shaw, ". . . he lost the ship deliberately and knowingly steaming into an ice field at the high speed he had coal for.").

Thomas Hardy was next. He composed a poem that was published in *The Fortnightly Review* and reprinted on newspaper front pages around the world. In "The Convergence of the Twain: Lines on the Loss of The *Titanic*," Hardy indicated as was often his wont, pride and vanity.

> And as the smart ship grew
> In stature, grace, and hue,
> In shadowy, silent distance grew the Iceberg too.
>
> Till the Spinner of the Years
> Said "Now!" And each one hears
> And consummation comes, and jars two hemispheres.

A *Times* editorial followed. It commented that the bad poets who had tried to pen verses about the *Titanic* should learn from Hardy. "Produced by a man of talent the poem is worth reading and studying, but it ought to serve as a dreadful warning for amateur poets." And there were literally hundreds of poets and song writers who wrote elegiac verses about the *Titanic*. Their output is remarkable for quantity, not for quality.

Novelist Joseph Conrad, arguably the best novelist of the sea and its perils ever to put pen to paper, quite willingly offered his opinion on the matter. In an essay in *The English Review* he railed at the hullabaloo the White Star Line had created about the *Titanic* before she sailed. "All the people on board existed under a sense of false security," he said. "The fact which seemed undoubted, that some of them actually were reluctant to enter the boats when told to do so, shows the strength of that falsehood." Long an opponent of the so-called big ship movement, Conrad found in the *Titanic* ample and justifying evidence for his righteous anger.

The public's taste for the story showed no sign of slackening. The formal reports were gradually filed for the public to read, but none of them—whether from the U.S. Senate, the British Board of Trade, or the editor of *Scientific American*—offered anything truly new. The exhaustive study in the *Scientific American* drew comparisons between the *Titanic* and the Cunard liner *Mauretania*, claiming the double-walls of the *Mauretania's* hulk would have prevented the catastrophic damage sustained by the *Titanic*. But the conclusions were all the same. In short, the ship was going too fast in the wrong place at the wrong time and after the damage was done there were insufficient safety devices to save the passengers and crew. There was quibbling in the English press, particularly over the leader of the Senate inquiry, Senator William Alden Smith, who had committed more than his share of faux pas and uttered many a malapropism as he questioned men more knowledgeable than he about the sea and its laws, but most everyone was agreed as to the facts of the matter.

As is the way with explosions like that surrounding the foundering of the *Titanic* and the legal brouhaha that followed, the dust finally settled and a silence ensued. Not that it was forgotten of course. There were sporadic bits of news. In July, an elderly ship captain in Baltimore reported having spoken to Captain E. J. Smith. (Smith's spectre was reported to have said, "Be good, shipmate, until we meet again.") Also in July a book by Lawrence Beesley, *The Loss of the S.S. Titanic*, was published. Another passenger's account, *The Truth About the Titanic* by Archibald Gracie, appeared the following year. Neither book was vastly popular. Occasional reports of all the pending legal suits continued until 1916 when they were finally disposed of. For the record the White Star Line paid the collected litigants $665,000 in damages, a negotiated settlement that rather pales beside the original claims of some $18 million.

It is also interesting that no individuals were forced to assume a share of the responsibility for the tragedy, particularly given the questionable conduct of J. Bruce Ismay. Ismay's wealth was said to be forty million dollars, reason enough perhaps not to tread on his toes, but standing behind Ismay was something even more powerful, the interests of J. P. Morgan that owned the *Titanic*. There had been, and would be, even presidents of the United States who stood in awe of this great banker. Had responsibility been assigned for the tragedy, Morgan stood to lose a huge amount of money in penalties and lawsuits.

The shock had worn off, and perhaps appropriately, a pall fell over the subject. Save for an occasional memoir (most especially Lightoller's in the thirties), little was added to the sorry and sordid tragedy of the *Titanic*. The *Titanic* rested thirteen thousand feet beneath the surface of the ocean, and the story was buried, too, though not nearly so deeply in the psyches of not only the survivors, but also the world that knew all too well what had happened. It simply wasn't necessary to bring the subject up. It was always there, a kind of objective correlative. To this day, in fact, invoking the name of the *Titanic* has an emotional value greater than all but a handful of history's most extraordinary events.

It was not until the 1950s that the *Titanic* stepped forth from its shadowy past. In 1955 Walter Lord's classic *A Night to Remember* brought the accident back to front and center. Not that the ensuing years hadn't felt the impact of the event. In fact, laws regarding sea safety and wireless regulations were instituted, and the International Ice Observation and Ice Patrol Services were initiated immediately after the disaster and continue to this day. But it was Lord who introduced an entire generation to a story they had not experienced but one that their parents could still feel better than they could describe.

A Night to Remember was, at its time and today, artfully constructed. The book moves cinematically from one scene to another, from one setting to another, all on board the *Titanic*. The effect is brilliant, and its you are there quality has been imitated many times but rarely equaled.

It was so effective a piece of writing and successful (it spent almost eight months on national best-seller lists), that it spawned a virtual revival. Television's *Kraft Theater* presented a live teleplay of the book, featuring one hundred and seven actors and thirty-one studio sets. In what has come to be called television's golden age, it was one of the high points. Claude Rains was the narrator and the young George Roy Hill the director. It was a triumphant success.

Two years later, the *Titanic* steamed into the movie theaters. In yet another adaptation of Lord's *A Night to Remember*, Kenneth More starred. (Bosley Crowther, in his review, called More, "the outstanding performer who play[ed] Lightoller with brisk assurance and stirring vitality. His evidences of competence, compassion, and unfailing bravery are in the best tradition of British seamanship.")

But it was the portrayal of *Californian* Captain Stanley Lord (no relation to Walter) who was most stirred by his casting in both the book and the movies as the obvious villain in the piece. Long since retired from the sea, he suddenly was heard from again. He had taken a captainship with the Lawther Latta Line after his dismissal by Leyland and served the rest of his long career traveling back and forth to South Africa. He called for a reopening of the Board of Trade investigation, which, like its American counterpart, had found him gulty of failing to take proper action the night of the disaster. The renaissance of interest in the *Titanic* had brought his part to the fore once again, and he embarked upon a campaign to clear his name.

At eighty-one he pursued his case. He won a valuable ally early on when the Mercantile Marine Service Association, which had declined to consider reopening his case in 1913, reversed its position and took his side in the matter. His petitions, however, were for naught, as the Board of Trade refused to air the case again. Lord died in 1962, at the age of eighty-four. The matter of his guilt or innocence is still a source of lively debate for some and also the subject of a book, *The Titanic and The Californian*, by Peter Padfield. The book is both dramatic and persuasive. Nevertheless, Lord still seems to most knowledgeable observers to be guilty as charged.

The ghost of the *Titanic* had appeared on television in a number of other guises. The first episode of a 1966 TV series called *Time Tunnel* delivered viewers to the decks of the *Titanic;* the well-remembered *Twilight Zone* began every show with Rod Serling's threatening voice invoking the *Titanic*'s name. *The Alcoa Hour, In Search of . . .* , *You Are There*, a Jacques Cousteau documentary, and even *Upstairs, Downstairs* recalled the *Titanic* (Lady Marjorie met with no pedestrian ending; as a first-class passenger, she went down with the *Titanic*).

Books too proliferate. Geoffrey Marcus's *The Maiden Voyage* was published in 1969 and may be the single most complete, detailed reconstruction of the events of April 14 and the aftermath. There is an oral history too, *The Story of the Titanic as Told by Its Survivors*, edited by Jack Winocour. And a book defending the American investigation, which had been so strongly criticized, particularly in England. *The Titanic: End of a Dream* contains a mixture of Marcus's and Lord's books, both a dramatic recreation of the events and an extended evaluation of the aftermath. The book, by Wyn Craig Wade, concludes with an intriguing wrap-up of what happened to the principals in the years between 1912 and 1979.

The most recent book to gain widespread popularity is *Raise the Titanic* by Clive Cussler. Although admittedly fantastic in conception, it didn't really matter. The book is paced in the modern manner, with a surprise turn of plot every chapter, and enough excitement for the most impatient reader. It accumulated all the accoutrements of a big book, with enormous popularity both among hardcover, paperback, and book club readers. And it became a "major" motion picture. Major, at least, to judge by its budget. English producer Lord Lew Grade spent a considerable fortune on the movie, a sum estimated at forty million dollars, more than four times the cost of the original *Titanic*. The film, to its backers' distress, sank into a sea of red ink.

So many songs have been written, TV shows broadcast, movies released, and books and magazine articles published that there seems little left to say. In fact, there is painfully little new to be found in anything made public since 1912. But a curiosity continues to linger.

There is still a sensitivity to the anguish the world experienced at the ship's sinking. In 1977 an English liquor manufacturer, International Distillers, developed a print advertising campaign for its Smirnoff vodka. It featured a photograph of a woman, afloat in the ocean, with a glass in her hand. "Well, they said anything could happen," she is saying. She is wearing a life jacket with the word *Titanic* on it.

When the ad appeared on billboards, in subways, and in magazines, there was an outcry. The British Advertising Standards Authority received a number of letters and complaints. As a result, the ad was withdrawn. Even sixty-five years later, emotions ran high.

In a sense, the sinking of the *Titanic* was a turning point for modernity. The *Titanic* symbolized a high point in industrial development, a height of luxury and wealth, a pinnacle in society's seemingly inexorable climb from animal to civilized dominant being. If progress was to be represented in a single accomplishment, then perhaps the *Titanic* was a perfect candidate. Before it sank, that is.

By the same token, then, nature is a great juggernaut, whose terrible, irresistible force demanded and received a terrible sacrifice of human life. The event's impact upon the world was at once to horrify and amaze all who heard but, one hopes, also to humble. At its most pedestrian the lesson is that when progress moves too quickly there is a price to be paid. Great leaps forward can outdistance the limitations and the logic of a world suddenly outdated.

"**O**nce a more or less specific location is known or suspected, one must then actually find the wreck, which is where the real work begins."

—Peter Throckmorton,
maritime archaeologist

CHAPTER V

OF SHIPWRECKS AND SALVAGE

The fates of ships are as varied as the vessels themselves. Some survive far beyond their utility as museum pieces, though usually their pristine condition is the result of reconstruction rather than careful use. Some ships die a natural death, finding themselves towed off to the junkheap where they are rent into hunks of metal for recycling.

The most interesting ships are those whose demise might be called unexpected. They are wrecks, the surprised victims of circumstance, Mother Nature, or man's folly. The *Titanic* may be the name that first comes to mind when the subject of shipwrecks is broached, but she is one of countless craft to founder.

Given that sailors are a profoundly suspicious lot, perhaps they would see some fearful appropriateness in the *Titanic*'s sinking, a kind of symmetry to the fate of the *Titanic* and her sister ship. It is as if she and the *Olympic* were cursed with bad luck. Only eight months before the *Titanic*'s precipitous end, her closest relation had an accident herself. The British cruiser *Hawke* stove a great hole in her side in a collision. A formal British inquiry into the event adjudged the *Hawke*'s captain innocent of any blame, ruling that the enormous liner had drawn the smaller ship out of its course through the suction of her engines.

The occurrence was repeated in virtually the same spot, though luckily without the same end, when the *Titanic* left Southhampton and pulled the *New York* from its moorings. The *Olympic*'s useful life was cut short, too, for she never fulfilled expectations after the *Titanic*'s sinking and the interference of World War I, and was tugged to the scrap heap a few years later.

The news of a ship having sunk is always dreaded, whether the ship is civilian or military, large or small, seagoing or designed for inland waterways. But there is something doubly shocking about a passenger ship sinking to the ineffable depths. In a sense it is not the loss of the hardy seamen that moves us most but rather the death of innocent passengers, for we identify with them most closely.

Though communications were very slow in the mid-nineteenth century, the news of the sinking of the *President* was no doubt a great shock. One of the first ships conceived, designed, and built specifically to be a passenger liner, it was also the first of the breed to sink. The *President* was the largest ship of its day—more than two hundred forty feet long—when it was launched in 1840. Details of its sinking, however, were nonexistent. It left New York on its third trip across the Atlantic and was never heard from again. There were no marconigrams to deliver the news of her fate.

A collision remarkably like the *Titanic*'s—save that the outcome was vastly different—took place in 1878. The steamship *Arizona* left New York and embarked northward on the long circle route through the North Atlantic. Four days out, a great crash threw the passengers from one side of the ship to the other.

They had struck an iceberg. The lights went out, and chairs and tables that had been screwed to the floor were ripped free. Passengers and crew alike ran to the boat deck. The lifeboats were readied.

There the resemblance to the *Titanic* tragedy ends. The *Arizona* had struck the berg head on, and the first thirty feet of her length crumpled. But her bulkheads held. Her captain, having surveyed the damage and having consulted with his crew, ordered the ship to back up. Off the ship went, bound for Newfoundland two hundred twenty miles away, ignominiously trailing her crumpled bow.

Icebergs only infrequently appear in the history of luxury ships, but an even more inappropriate fate is common in the annals of passenger-ship history. The great graceful liners, whose designers devoted as much energy to installing creature comforts as to economy or safety, have often found themselves commandeered for military duty. How ill suited the military and the passenger ships are to a partnership has been demonstrated time and again, though much of the evidence lies beneath the seven seas.

In World War I, two liners, the German Hamburg–South America Line's *Cap Trafalgar* and Cunard's *Carmania*, actually met in combat. While the *Cap Trafalgar*'s artillery did manage to land enough shells on the *Carmania* to make a shambles of her bridge, it was the German ship that capsized and sank.

As warships, most liners were totally ill suited. They were vulnerable, given their weak superstructures and hulls, and costly to run, coal being particularly precious in wartime. But as hospital and troop ships, they proved their mettle. Many of the great liners were put to use in wartime, including the great Cunard queens, *Elizabeth* and *Mary*. The *Queen Elizabeth* saw wartime service before she ever carried a paying passenger. The tradition of using passenger ships in wartime is honored even today, as the recent Falkland Islands crisis attests, with the *Queen Elizabeth II* having been commandeered by the British Navy for duty as a troop ship.

Some lines tried to maintain passenger service in World War I, even after hostilities had begun. The liners of neutral countries gained considerable business during the early months of the war, since most of the German and British ships that had dominated the marketplace during peacetime had been put to other uses. The Dutch Holland–America and the American IMM lines made huge profits.

The undermanned Cunard and White Star Lines did try to maintain some semblance of business as usual. Thus, the *Lusitania* traveled between New York and Liverpool—until May 7, 1915.

The morning it sailed out of New York harbor for the last time, the newspapers carried a warning from the Imperial German Embassy in Washington warning that English ships were "liable to destruction." The *Lusitania* was the last of the large liners still operating on the North Atlantic under any flag, but her captain was confident she could outrun any submarine. Her passengers comforted themselves that she would have the protection of a cruiser escort when she reached the European war zone.

Unfortunately, her escort never appeared. A U-boat did, and a single torpedo struck the *Lusitania*'s starboard side. A second explosion, apparently caused by the ignition of contraband munitions, blew out much of her double-bottomed bow. Twenty minutes later she sank to the ocean floor just south of Ireland, taking a human life toll of twelve hundred.

Some historians have argued that the *Lusitania* was deliberately offered up to tempt the Germans and to hasten America's entry into the war (one hundred twenty-eight of the twelve hundred were American). Whatever the politics of the matter, it was again a lifeboat failure that added to the loss of life. The ship listed far to starboard, and most of the lifeboats on that side swung so far from the ship as to be dangerous to enter.

Another of the best remembered accidents at sea was due not to man's malevolence to man, but rather to a still unexplained moment of carelessness.

During World War II, the toll taken of passenger ships was heavy. Only hours before Britain declared war on Germany the *Athenia* was sunk by German torpedoes just off the Irish coast. One hundred twelve people died. In the course of the war many other liners were sunk, including the German *Bremen* and England's *Empress of Britain*. The Italian line lost both the *Rex* and the *Conte di Savoia*, so after the war a new flagship was in order. The *Andrea Doria* was launched in 1952. Her story, too, has aspects that are reminiscent of the *Titanic's*. Her design incorporated all the latest safety devices, as well as some that had become traditional. She had radar and also watertight compartments and a double hull. The hype that her launching occasioned made the most of the attributes.

On the foggy night of June 25, 1956, her radar was a necessity. Bound for New York, she was proceeding with seeming care when a ship loomed ahead. It was the Swedish liner *Stockholm*. If the *Andrea Doria* had followed the usual nautical procedures, she would have passed the *Stockholm* on her port side without incident. The two ships were in radio contact, and all seemed well.

In a bizarre and still unexplained moment, the exquisite Italian liner sliced into the path of the *Stockholm*. The bow of the Swedish ship, which was reinforced to withstand the icefloes common to Scandinavian waters, ripped a seven-story-high gash in the *Andrea Doria*.

One shocked passenger on the Italian ship awoke on the deck of the *Stockholm*, her cabinmates killed by the crash. In the next few hours, all but fifty-one of the more than seventeen hundred on board the *Andrea Doria* escaped, only to watch the listing liner gradually capsize and then lumber out of sight. A straggly group of deck chairs floated on the spot where she disappeared—a pathetic remembrance of her luxury.

Ironically, the true predecessor to the much ballyhooed "safe" ships like the *Andrea Doria* and the *Titanic* was the *Great Eastern*. Launched in 1857, she was *five* times the size of any vessel then afloat (the *Titanic* only outweighed the *Olympic* by a thousand tons). Intended to travel to the Far East, she was capable of carrying enough coal for the entire ten-thousand-mile trip.

The *Great Eastern* was fifty years ahead of her time. She had an iron hull and watertight compartments. She also had two kinds of power, though rather than two kinds of engines like the *Titanic* she had both paddlewheels and a propellor. She was the first to use a steam-powered steering gear, which allowed her wheelhouse to be moved toward the bow, so the helmsman could better see where he was pointing the ship. Her tremendous size also allowed her to carry enough cable to cross the ocean—and she laid the first successful telegraph cable across the Atlantic.

Like many things ahead of their time, the *Great Eastern* never found a comfortable niche and so her end was rather like a strong man who gives up legitimate labor and retires to the circus. She ended her days as an amusement hall, a tourist trap covered with billboards. But she never besmirched her reputation by allowing Mother Nature to swallow her.

Once a ship abandons the ocean's surface for the netherworld, a whole new universe of people becomes interested in them. No longer are they fawned over by swabbies. Tourists and travelers cease to hand over large sums of money to sail on them.

Wrecked ships can be the source of entertainment, profit, or knowledge. In a sense men like Jack Grimm and Peter Gimbel, the heir to the Gimbels department store fortune, try for all three. (Gimbel, in the summer of 1981, along with a professional crew of divers, dove to the wreck of the *Andrea Doria*. He brought a safe from the ship to the surface, and intends to open it on network television for the world to share in the moment of revelation.) For amateur divers, the lure of a shipwreck lies in the adventure, the thrill of discovery. The professionals want more: They search for history or dollars, or both.

They are the maritime archaeologists and the salvage companies. One man who was both, although by proxy rather than in person, was Lord Elgin. In 1802 the brig *Mentor* broke up on the rocks at the entrance to St. Nicholas Bay in the Aegean Sea. Her primary cargo was seventeen cases of marble. The marble was the frieze from the Parthenon taken by Lord Elgin. His divers spent two full years searching sixty feet down and salvaging the relics which are now proudly displayed in the British Museum.

Strictly speaking, the English peer was not a maritime archaeologist, although he was clearly interested in matters historical. If one had to classify him, however, he would have to be placed in the camp of the salvors, men who go to the ocean floor for profit, to resurrect what ships or cargo can be brought up and resold.

Maritime archaeology is the systematic recovery and scientific investigation of material evidence of past ships and seafaring. Few areas of human endeavor have so little physical evidence to show for their accomplishments as does the history of naval architecture. Ships, unlike abandoned houses or buried treasure, do not remain essentially intact and accessible, unless, of course, the finders are looking deep into the sea.

Though it is next to impossible to date the beginning of any academic discipline, most experts date the birth of maritime archaeology as being 1900. The same breed of men who had served Lord Elgin's expedition (some were actually descendants of Elgin's diving crew) were laboring at their life's work, diving for sponges. Two boats of divers worked on the lce side of the island of Antikythera, once again in the Aegean, as they waited for a storm to blow over.

One diver, his head and upper body adorned with the copper helmet that had come into use since the salvage of the *Mentor*, worked one hundred eighty feet down. Suddenly, he rose to the surface, too fast, well before the time period his captain, Dimitrios Kondos, had alloted as "safe" to be underwater.

He babbled when they removed his helmet. His words were entirely incoherent at first, but when his companions and Kondos calmed him enough that they could understand him, his words still seemed insane. He went on about women with syphilis, and horses, and more naked women.

Kondos himself dived to see what he could find. He came back, within the allotted five minutes, bringing with him a man's hand. It was a right hand, heavy and sickly green.

"Statues," he said to his dumbfounded crew. "Statues, you cuckold idiots. A whole shipload of statues." Rarely have such crude words offered so dramatic an opportunity for science and history. And the women didn't have syphilis, of course, but had been corroded by years in the sea.

The provenance of the wreck and its cargo of more than thirty statues is still unclear, although it is generally thought to have been Roman in origin, and to date from the first half of the first century B.C. (The ship probably contained treasures captured by the Romans in Greece, the spoils of war from victories in Sulla in 86 B.C.) To date the marine archaeologists have not resurrected the structure of the ship, which rests under a few inches of sand. But perhaps in ensuing years, with some systematic work on the wreck, its exact identity and destination will be discovered.

Regardless, it was a fantastic find. Not only were the statues raised to the surface, but other objects, including an early mechanical calculator, were discovered. The value of the Antikythera wreck, both artistically and archaeologically, is immeasurable. But perhaps its true importance was that it demonstrated the great potential of underwater archaeology. The wreck was untouched by human hands, the mnemonic failure of the scribes, or the relative ignorance of historians attempting to reconstruct it. The ship had plummeted to the bottom, frozen in time, a microcosm of a culture. Only rarely is such an accidental time capsule to be found ashore. The Pompeiis are few and far between; shipwrecks like that at Antikythera are uncommon, but not unique.

There were other major maritime discoveries of antiquities before and after Kondos brought the Antikytheran statues to the surface. In the seventeenth century men had descended the depths in diving bells, in the eighteenth in enclosed barrels, and finally in the nineteenth in the hard-hat diving gear used by Kondos and his men. But the science of maritime archaeology awaited one revolutionary invention and the organizational abilities of one man before it truly came of age.

In 1943 Jacques-Yves Cousteau, then a French Navy officer, and an engineer named Emile Gagnan created the first practical aqualung for the French Navy. It allowed the diver to roam the sea independent of his support ship, unlike the old hard-hat diving gear that required an air line to link the diver to a compressor in the ship above. The aqualung diver is more mobile, as the new equipment is far lighter than the old and vastly less cumbersome. The aqualung's introduction was nothing less than revolutionary.

Cousteau's contribution is far more than as simply co-inventor of the aqualung. He founded the Undersea Research Group, which combined the skills of geologists, biologists, and oceanographers. He taught scientists to dive, so they could apply their expertise themselves beneath the surface, rather than rely upon sponge divers to act as their eyes and hands.

Cousteau directed the first serious attempt to systematically investigate a classical wreck using the new apparatus. Beginning in 1952, Cousteau and his men moored under the cliffs of a rocky islet near Marseilles called the Grand Congloue. The wreck below dated from the first half of the second century B.C., and was a treasure trove of amphoras and black glazed dishes. Teams of divers worked for five years and eventually recovered some *two hundred tons* of materials, including lead ship fittings, planks, domestic pottery from the galley, anchors, and a miscellany of other millenia-old goods.

Today, marine archaeologists look down their noses at the Grand Congloue expedition since it was not adequately controlled from an archaeological standpoint. No drawings or photographs were made to record the positions of the treasures found. But Cousteau's contribution cannot be understated. He demonstrated it was possible for teams of divers to spend thousands of hours safely underwater, and that the systematic, piecemeal excavation of a wreck was not only possible but practical.

The next seminal figure in the evolution of maritime archaeology is George Bass. An American who trained as an archaeologist on land, he brought to maritime work the discipline that was standard operating procedure on terra firma.

Bass's first law was that the archaeologists, not the divers, are in charge. His second was that the entire excavation process had to be subjected to precise recordkeeping procedures. That way, even the smallest bit of physical evidence could later be located precisely with respect to the other recovered artifacts. Then, when the time came to play jigsaw puzzle and reassemble the pieces on dry land, the invaluable plan made it possible. In a very real sense, Bass made the appellation *science* appropriate to the previously hit-or-miss practice of maritime archaeology.

Until recent years, maritime archeologists concentrated on older wrecks. Since much is known of the shipbuilder's art as practiced since the mid-seventeenth century, the most energy was devoted to studying older ships. Occasionally, a mid-eighteenth century wreck was the subject of their curiosity, such as some Dutch traders and even some Revolutionary warships. But rarely were the ships more recent.

In the last decade or so things have begun to change. In the mid-seventies the old ironclads, the *Monitor* and the *Merrimack*, were both found and expeditions to raise them were much discussed. To date neither has been brought to the surface, and it appears that the remains of the *Monitor* may be so fragile that they can never be brought to the surface, at least in anything other than

Jack Grimm dockside in Boston (Credit: Anita Brosius)

R/V *Gyre* leaving Woods Hole harbor, June 28, 1981 (Credit: Anita Brosius)

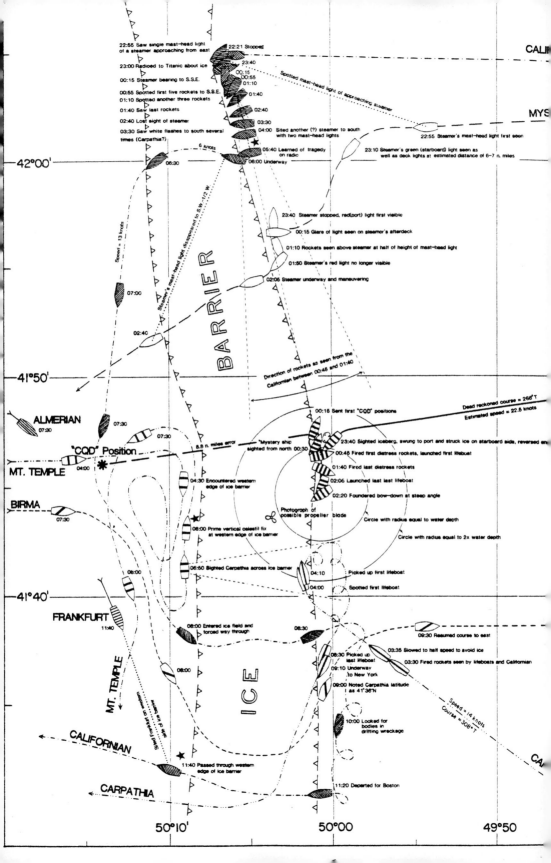

22:55 Saw single mast-head light of a steamer approaching from east

23:00 Radioed to Titanic about ice

00:15 Steamer bearing to S.S.E.

00:55 Spotted first five rockets to S.S.E.

01:10 Spotted another three rockets

01:40 Saw last rockets

02:40 Lost sight of steamer

03:30 Saw white flashes to south several times (Carpathia?)

22:21 Stopped

23:40
00:15
00:55
01:10
01:40
02:40
03:30
04:00 Sited another (?) steamer to south with two mast-head lights

05:40 Learned of tragedy on radio

06:00 Underway

CALI

MYS

Spotted mast-head light of approaching steamer

22:55 Steamer's mast-head light first seen

23:10 Steamer's green (starboard) light seen as well as deck lights at estimated distance of 6–7 n. miles

−42°00′

6 knots

06:30

Speed = 13 knots

Steamer's mast-head light disappeared to S.S.W.-1/2 W.

BARRIER

07:00

02:40

23:40 Steamer stopped, red (port) light first visible

00:15 Glare of light seen on steamer's afterdeck

01:10 Rockets seen above steamer at half of height of mast-head light

01:50 Steamer's red light no longer visible

02:05 Steamer underway and maneuvering

−41°50′

Direction of rockets as seen from the Californian between 00:45 and 01:40

Dead reckoned course = 266° T

Estimated speed = 22.5 knots

00:15 Sent first "CQD" positions

23:40 Sighted iceberg, swung to port and struck ice on starboard side, reversed en

00:45 Fired first distress rockets, launched first lifeboat

01:40 Fired last distress rockets

02:06 Launched last last lifeboat

02:20 Foundered bow-down at steep angle

"Mystery ship" sighted from north 00:30

8.8 n. miles error

ALMERIAN
07:30

07:30

07:30

"CQD" Position

MT. TEMPLE
04:00

BIRMA
07:30

04:30 Encountered western edge of ice barrier

06:00

06:50 Sighted Carpathia across ice barrier

Photograph of possible propeller blade

Circle with radius equal to water depth

Circle with radius equal to 2x water depth

08:00 Prime vertical celestial fix at western edge of ice barrier

04:10 Picked up first lifeboat

04:00 Spotted first lifeboat

−41°40′

FRANKFURT
11:40

08:00 Entered ice field and forced way through

08:00

08:30

MT. TEMPLE

09:30 Resumed course to east

03:35 Slowed to half speed to avoid ice

03:30 Fired rockets seen by lifeboats and Californian

08:30 Picked up last lifeboat

09:10 Underway to New York

09:00 Noted Carpathia latitude as 41°36′N

Speed = 14 knots
Course = 308° T

CALIFORNIAN

10:00 Looked for bodies in drifting wreckage

CA

11:40 Passed through western edge of ice barrier

11:20 Departed for Boston

CARPATHIA

50°10′   50°00′   49°50′

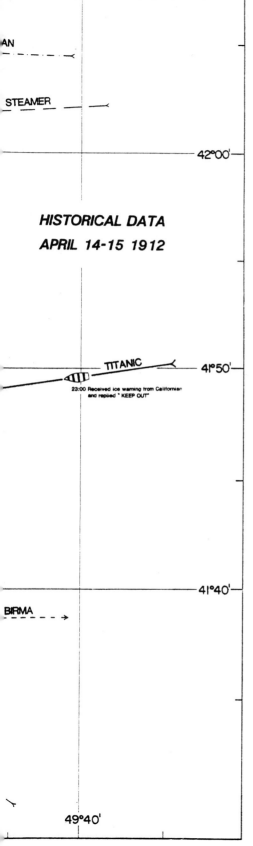

AN

STEAMER

42°00'

HISTORICAL DATA
APRIL 14-15 1912

TITANIC   41°50'

23:00 Received ice warning from Californian
and replied " KEEP OUT"

41°40'

BIRMA

49°40'

Map showing area where the *Titanic* sank,
with inferred tracks of ships
in the vicinity of the accident

(Credit: Titanic 1981, Inc.)

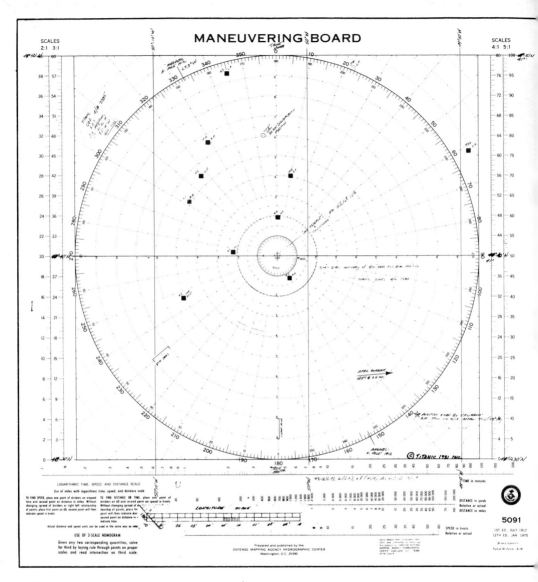

Maneuvering Board

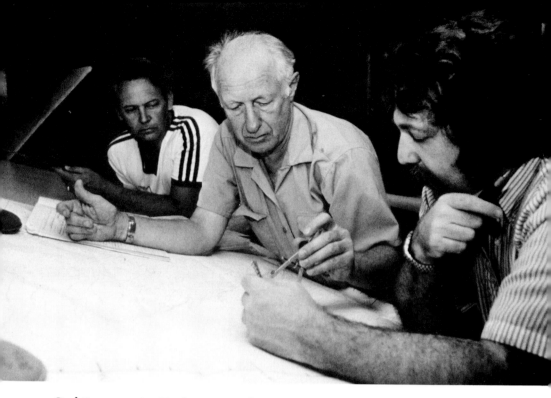

Carl Lowenstein, Fred Spiess and Mike Harris planning transponder deployment (Credit: Anita Brosius)

Sea floor map showing approximate area where *Titanic* sank (Credit: Anita Brosius)

Deep Tow being prepared during heavy
seas (Credit: Anita Brosius)

Mike Harris filming Deep Tow deck preparations.
(Credit: Anita Brosius)

Deep Tow deployment. (Credit: Anita Brosius)

John Jain adjusting Deep Tow electronics (Credit: Anita Brosius)

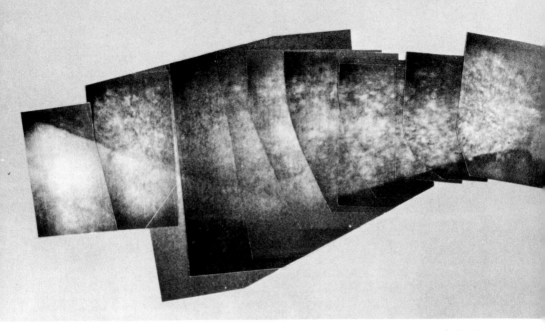

A slide of the mosaic made of the "propeller" sighted on the trip back to port (Credit: Anita Brosius)

Blade of one of the propellers from the *Oceanic*, sister ship of the *Titanic*. Note the leaching, pitting, and similar shape to the mosaic blade (Credit: Dundee Courier, Scotland)

the smallest of pieces. The *Merrimack* may yet be saved, however. Author Clive Cussler maintains the *Merrimack* lies closer to the surface than the *Monitor*, possibly in better condition. Cussler says that portions as large as nine tons may be salvageable.

An important piece of one nineteenth-century ship has been not only brought to the surface, but all the way to one of the Smithsonian museums: the engine of the ore ship *Indiana*. Rediscovered in 1975 in Lake Superior, it had sat in one hundred twenty feet of cold fresh water since 1853. Remarkably intact, it was brought up by two Navy outfits, one from Little Creek, Virginia, one from the Chicago Naval Reserve. Under the direction of two Smithsonian officials, the boiler, pipes, pumps, and other mechanisms were brought to the surface.

The *Indiana*'s engine offers a unique opportunity to historians, since it is not only in excellent condition, but also is essentially the same as it was when it was built in 1848. Unlike other engines—extant marine and land that date from the same period—this one was not subject to tinkering in ensuing years to improve it. It is in authentic condition, only slightly deteriorated from oxidation since it went to the lake's bottom. The ship was sunk when its propellor shaft punctured her bottom, and luckily, all hands got off safely and rowed to shore. Now, more than a century later, the steam engine will shortly go on display at the Museum of History and Technology at the Smithsonian Institution.

One key factor in the new interest in more recent shipwrecks is the emerging technology. It is now possible to accomplish resurrections not even conceivable in years past. One spectacular example is the Swedish warship *Wasa*. Although the *Wasa* is by no means a modern ship—she sank in 1628, apparently because of a fundamental design flaw that caused her to capsize on her maiden voyage—her raising was a wondrous accomplishment. Tunnels were dug under the wreck so that cables could be wrapped around her hull. She was then raised to the surface, and situated upon a concrete pontoon. Such ingenuity and the worm-free waters of the Baltic have made Swedish maritime archaeology among the most accomplished in the world.

The precision of the maritime archaeologists stands in sharp relief to the labors of the salvors, then and now. To a trained, professional diver, as well as to the ship's captain and other men involved in figuring profit, time is money. The goal is simple: Get to the surface whatever cargo can be got there. Or, if the goal is to save the ship, then to do it as quickly, safely, and efficiently as possible.

Before the precise definition of Bass and company, the line of demarcation between salvage and archaeology was blurred, though there was nothing unclear about the salvage of the wreck of the steamer *Alphonse XII*. In 1885 it sank to a depth of one hundred sixty feet in the English Channel. A salvage diver named Alexander Lambert recovered ninety thousand pounds of gold from her strong room, but he paid a terrible price. Struck by the dreaded bends, he lived out his life paralyzed.

The cargo of the *Egypt* had the same lure to salvors when it went down following a collision in the Bay of Biscay. Today, the depth of 396 feet would not be impossible for divers breathing a special mixture of oxygen and other gases, but in 1922 her five tons of gold and two tons of silver were beyond human hands.

But not beyond the reach of technology. An Italian salvage crew went down to the ship in observation chambers. The metal of the chambers protected them from the weight of the water, and they breathed air at ordinary atmospheric pressure. From their little bell jars they lowered explosives, blew up the ship, then "fished" for the gold and silver with remote control claws.

Not only are the goals of the salvor and the archaeologist different, but also their audiences are different as well. While the archaeologist pursues knowledge for its own sake, and communicates it to an academic few or, occasionally, a lay public, the salvor is a businessman whose primary contact is with the insurance companies. Insurors who stand to lose millions of dollars in reimbursements are those most interested in resurrecting ships and cargo.

Sometimes the goal is to salvage ships for the scrap value of their steel. That was the case with perhaps the largest salvage venture ever, the raising of the German High Seas Fleet. Scuttled by the Germans in 1919 in order to prevent the seventy-two ships from falling into British hands, the hulks stood in Scapa Flow, a sea basin north of Scotland in the Orkneys. It took years, but dozens of the ships were salvaged.

The old-fashioned variety of salvage practiced by Lord Elgin is still seen today. Salvage of cargo, not only gold, but oil and other goods, has increased in status in recent years. Nuclear weapons, in particular, have been the objects of salvors. In fact, it was the little submarine *Aluminaut*, which Jack Grimm planned to use on another expedition to the *Titanic*, that recovered a hydrogen bomb that had dropped into the ocean off the coast of Spain.

In February 1960 a KC-125 and a B-52 collided in midair, and two hydrogen bombs came tumbling from the sky. Had either exploded it would have been a tragedy of unimaginable proportions. One of them landed in a farmer's tomato patch in the town of Palomares, and the farmer was given a packet of money, partly because it is an undeniable inconvenience to have an H-bomb land in your yard, but mostly, it was suspected, to keep him from talking too much about the incident.

The other bomb went down in the ocean, and because nearby U.S. Navy ships (including a nuclear submarine) lacked the sonar capabilities to find it, the privately owned *Aluminaut* was commissioned to help conduct the critical search. Also involved was the *Alvin*, another submersible, which operates out of Woods Hole, and a cubmarine, which could not descend below six hundred feet (the *Aluminaut* has gone to fifteen thousand feet).

It took almost two tension-filled months, while Russian ships monitored the operation from a distance, to find the bomb. Even then it was brought to the surface in the most frightening fashion:

by accident. A grapple inadvertently snagged the parachute to which the bomb was attached and pulled it to the top. The bomb was beneath twenty-seven hundred feet of water.

The greatest, most challenging kind of salvage of all is to bring the ship, especially a large ship, back up to the surface—and to bring it to the surface as nearly intact as possible.

There are a number of ways to bring a ship back up. One is to patch her holes and, if her deck is above the surface, pump out the water and refloat her. Another is to attach pontoons to the wreck to float her to the surface. A third method is to lift a wreck with wires passed under her, as the Swedish maritime archaeologists did with the *Wasa*. A final method, most useful with submarines because of their peculiar structure, is to fill the ship with compressed air, which will provide a buoyancy to bring her to the surface. This method is especially good for wrecks at deep depths.

The number of ships that have gone to the bottom far outnumber those that have been brought back up. For some, there is an obvious reason. For example, the S.S. *Artemia* was sunk in the harbor of Milos, Greece, during World War II. Allied aircraft torpedoed her in 1942 and delivered her cargo of munitions to the muddy sea bottom rather than to Rommel's Africa Corps. To this day, she lies one hundred eighty feet down, virtually untouched. Estimates are that she will remain essentially intact for decades more before disintegrating. And with her hazardous cargo, her gradual decline isn't likely to be sped up by the interference of human hands. She is truly a time bomb, waiting for a careless diver to detonate her.

For others, there isn't sufficient potential gain to justify the enormous costs of salvage. In still other cases, it would seem that the technology is not up to task. While bathyspheres and bathyscaphes have been down thousands of feet, the ocean is up to seven miles deep. A diver breathing mixed gases (mixed gases are those that are carefully blended to reduce the content of nitrogen, so as to reduce the severity of the "bends," also known as nitrogen narcosis), may reach roughly nine hundred feet. Certain submersibles like the *Aluminaut* go much farther. It would appear, however, that careful, accurate archaeology is impossible much beyond a few hundred feet and even clumsy, inexact salvage has a lower limit of thousands of feet.

At least that was the thinking until the advent of the *Glomar Explorer*. That ship, a 36,000-ton, 618-foot-long "platform" with a derrick amidships, was unique. And built, it seems, with CIA monies for Howard Hughes and for espionage purposes.

The story has been aired at length in the press, although very few of its many aspects have been satisfactorily confirmed. The essence of the tale seems to be that in 1968, a Russian submarine went down in the northwest Pacific. The Russians didn't know exactly where, but U.S. Navy reconnaissance devices were able to place the wreck within a few square miles.

Project Jennifer was born and with its salvage entered a new age. Previously, the occasional military plane crash had led to the salvage of nuclear weapons from the sea, and available equipment like the *Aluminaut* had been sufficient for the tasks. Suddenly, an assignment of unprecedented difficulty loomed.

The sub was in sixteen thousand feet of water, far below the reach of any diver or even submarine. The sub, though light by surface shipping standards, probably weighed some four thousand tons. Impossible as the task seemed, it was worth risking a great deal to accomplish. With the superpowers matching wits, each monitors the other's accumulation of armaments. In the never-ending striving to quantify what the enemy is capable of, the sunken sub promised to be a veritable treasure chest of previously unattainable information.

Little of the U.S.'s knowledge of the U.S.S.R.'s weapons systems and intelligence-gathering devices is first hand. Most of it is photographic, typically pictures taken of Soviet missiles from satellites, or simply intelligence gathered on reconnaissance flights over re-entry sights of Soviet warheads. There were thought to be three nuclear-tipped missiles aboard the sunken sub. In addition recovery of the entire sub was thought to mean that the cipher machine and code books would also be captured. There were dozens of other incentives, including the fact that the U.S. Navy had never had the opportunity to handle a Soviet sub or to subject the steel in the sub's hull to metallurgical analysis. If the Soviet sub could be salvaged, U.S. intelligence would gain a quantum advantage over the opposition.

So the CIA embarked upon Project Jennifer. The cost is estimated to have been 350 million dollars. The Project employed more than four thousand people. And it was so shrouded in secrecy that even today, almost a decade and a half after its inception, few hard facts are known. In fact *Science* magazine's coverage of the recovery of the sub relied on the writings and illustrations of Willard Bascom, the Director of the Southern California Coastal Water Research Project, and a leading innovator in deep-sea research technology—and he wasn't even involved in the project. Although the manufacturer of the *Glomar Explorer* disclaims any debt to Bascom, patents and designs of his bear a considerable resemblance to the reported configuration of the Project Jennifer equipment.

Exactly what happened is unclear. When asked what the *Glomar Explorer* accomplished, a CIA spokesman responded, "That's a non-starter around here." But the most commonly heard reports have it that the sub was lifted, intact, off the ocean floor, and that part way to the surface two-thirds of the sub broke off and tumbled back to the floor of the Pacific Ocean. No code books or nuclear warheads were recovered, but perhaps a torpedo or two were.

There is still debate as to whether even this was possible, given the capabilities of other extant salvage ships, the largest of which is capable of bringing up only fifty tons from the depths in which the Russian sub is mired, rather than the four thousand tons the

Soviet sub is reported to have weighed. The precise nature of the expedition, what it accomplished, and the technical details of its equipment will probably only become public knowledge a good many years hence, so for now the curious layman must content himself with the knowledge that enormous sums were invested, presumably for some gain in knowledge about how to accomplish such feats, even if the sub wasn't raised for great intelligence gains.

Indirectly, the *Glomar Explorer* brings us back to the *Titanic*. The *Glomar Challenger,* an elder but smaller sister ship of the *Explorer,* was built in the same shipyard several years before for oceanographic research. One of the scientists who conducted studies from its deck was on board the *Gyre.* Bill Ryan was perhaps the most interesting person aboard on our venture. I am sure he is the perfect teacher for young would-be scientists, mainly because he possesses the skill to put into clear, concise language even the most complicated concepts. Science, when Ryan speaks about it, is something to be enjoyed, not to be frightened of or intimidated by.

After taking a degree in physics from Williams College in Williamstown, Massachusetts, he landed a job at Woods Hole where he worked to develop seismic profiling: bouncing echoes off the seafloor and into the seafloor to learn how old the ocean is and whether it is permanent. A few years later, he was impressed by a lecture he heard delivered by Bruce Heezen, a pioneer in mapping the ocean floor. Heezen talked about the rift valley in the middle of the Atlantic, the place where the Atlantic is being torn open, suggesting that even today continents are continuing to drift.

"I was intrigued by the continental drift debate," Ryan says, "and knew I would have to study geology if I was going to make any contribution to the issue."

Enrolling at Columbia, Ryan studied under Heezen. He

measured how hot the crust of the earth was on the ocean floor, and found the greatest heat was near the crack, which meant that was where the action was: volcanoes.

Ryan discovered that the ocean floor near continents "are flatter than a billiard table and covered with sediments more than a mile thick." Mighty mountains and ridges are buried entirely by sediments.

He was often at sea, "because the answer to so many puzzles is out there." In the Northern Mediterranean he discovered a young mountain chain and learned more about how the crushing of oceans against continents causes the creation of mountains. In the Eastern Mediterranean he found an underwater mountain chain that was in the process of formation and chose it as the subject of his doctoral dissertation.

Ryan was able to date the age of various oceans and to calculate precisely how fast they were expanding. "The oldest ocean," he says, "is the part of the Atlantic just off New York. Oceans become younger as you move to the center, and North America and Africa were once joined. Once you could walk down what is now Wall Street and after a few hundred miles you'd be in Mauretania."

Ryan bursts with fascinating tidbits. Tanzania is currently separating from Zimbabwe. The Mount St. Helens eruption was caused by the Northeast Pacific sliding under the coasts of Oregon, Washington, and British Columbia. Oceans expand six feet every sixty years. The Black Sea was nothing but an isolated lake during the last Ice Age, but it became connected to the Mediterranean nine thousand years ago when huge ice sheets in North America, Russia, and the Scandinavian countries melted, causing the water to rise an astounding three hundred fifty feet.

In 1970 Ryan studied the Mediterranean in the *Glomar Challenger* and learned that five million years ago this great sea was a vast depressed basin, nothing more than a series of small lakes. It became a huge body of water only after a catastrophe (perhaps a powerful earthquake) created an opening to the Atlantic Ocean which then flowed into what we know as the Mediterranean. "The true historians," Ryan says, "are geologists. We piece together history not from past accounts of events we didn't witness and can't verify, but from incontrovertible scientific data."

At times scientific disciplines overlap. Oceanography, geology, and even archaeology sometimes coincide. One as yet unexplored example of such is Atlantis. Ryan says he knows where the legendary lost city is. It's in the middle of the Aegean Sea, he says, and known as Santorini Islands. He believes it was demolished in 1450 B.C. by a huge eruption that could have been as much as a thousand times more powerful than what occurred at Mount St. Helens.

The center of Santorini simply collapsed and sank to the bottom of the ocean. "However," says Ryan, "there might never have been a Western Civilization if the wind had been blowing in a different direction that day." Huge clouds of volcanic ash were carried over to Crete and wiped out all agriculture. King Midas's palace was ruined by the ash, and the people of Crete fled to Greece.

But what if the wind had been blowing differently?

"Probably everyone would have migrated to Lebanon or Africa," says Ryan. "Probably no Western Civilization."

The destruction of Atlantis, says Ryan, could also explain the biblical story of the parting of the Red Sea for Moses. The eruption took place—worked out by the dating of sediments and archaeology—at a time when the Israeli nation was in captivity in Egypt. Huge tidal waves would have resulted, which probably would have caused the Red Sea to recede.

Ryan can indeed entertain even the most jaded listener. He was able to verify Pliny's account of the eruption of Mount Vesuvius in A.D. 79 and the destruction of Pompeii. His varied academic pursuits and unquestioned scientific credentials lent confidence to the belief that we would find the *Titanic*.

Spiess and Ryan and the other scientists gave me and the other laymen on board the *Gyre* a sense that what we were aiming to do was not only possible but even feasible. The utter competence of our crew seemed all the more assuring when compared to a previously announced venture to the *Titanic* site.

In 1970 a group of salvage enthusiasts in Baldock, England, announced that they were planning to raise the *Titanic*. The spokesman for the outfit, Douglas Wooley, was quoted as saying, "We have reached the final stage, to get the photographs of the vessel from the bottom of the sea. This will cost about £10,000, which we have been promised by a firm in West Germany."

Mr. Wooley's company, Titantic and Seawise Salvage Company, apparently lost its promised funding and floundered for the next few years, in and out of courtrooms. He had planned to raise the ship "with electronic equipment" and to accomplish it within a year, for a mere 4.8 million dollars. Little has been heard from him in recent years.

Perhaps Wooley had beaten us to the site in secret and found the *Titanic*. I doubt it. From the little I know of his plan from newspaper accounts, he is an idealist, looking to find the great ship.

I suspect the *Titanic* is beyond the reach of Mr. Wooley. But given men like Spiess and Ryan and the technology they and others pioneered, I was confident that we would succeed.

"*I just want to give it my best shot. Once she was written off as lost forever.*"

—Don Armand,
   captain of the *Gyre*

CHAPTER VI

THE FRUITLESS SEARCH

A full-fledged storm bounced our little *Gyre* in the water, but no one, except Harris, became seasick, because Drury had passed out pills the night before. In the galley over coffee Jake Vanderkim suggested portholes be painted with sunny scenes so we could believe conditions were better than they were.

"Gusts forty to forty-five miles an hour this morning," said Captain Don Armand. "Down to twenty to twenty-five now."

Seen out of the portholes the sea was snarling, dirty gray whacking the boat. Silverware and dishes slid crashing off the bolted-down galley tables. "Take a look at the lab," suggested Farre.

Only Lowenstein was there, bewildered, precious equipment willy-nilly across the floor, the place absolute chaos. The floor was carpeted with computer readout paper, and odds and ends of paraphernalia rolled out of control like berserk bowling balls.

Evidently no one, save Lowenstein, believed the battle was worth waging.

In the galley people agreed this was a good day to stay indoors. Jake Vanderkim said he thought a lot of unsolved murders occurred aboard ships on days like this; it was an easy matter to push someone overboard. The isolation of being at sea, and the time available to nurture grudges, added a man-made danger to what nature already contributed.

"We could start the game early," Grimm suggested, grimacing as he unsteadily made his way into the galley.

"Good idea," said Mike Harris.

This former Eagle Scout pondered the morality of church bingo games. It was out of character for him to encourage gambling, but his reason became clear soon enough. "Part of the flavor of the expedition," he said, "is the nightly card game. This is a good time, with everything stopped by the weather, to film it for the movie."

"Excellent thinking, Mike," said Grimm, reaching for an unopened deck of cards. These were sandwiched between cereal boxes on a ledge underneath the porthole, and it had not yet occurred to anyone to speculate about who had the foresight to stock a supply large enough for a casino.

Grimm really did think it was "excellent thinking." He had profound respect for efficient use of time, and the movie crew, he felt, had so far been mostly dead weight. Taking motion picture shots of the game accomplished two things at once on this miserable day: It produced footage for the movie, and gave him the chance to add numbers to the IOUs from various poker games.

"To make it true to life," said Harris to Grimm, "we should show you winning. Maybe we should arrange a set-up hand."

"That's all right," said Grimm, shuffling the now-opened deck, "it will be true enough."

This should have been a warning, but instead it served to stir competitive juices. Bobby Blanco did several quick sit-ups, a

couple of knee bends, and businesslike and determined, sat opposite the tycoon. Burris took his accustomed spot on the side.

"I'll get Petrik up," said Harris.

"That boy can sleep a lot, can't he?" said Grimm, a certain
admiration in his voice.

"Get the game going. It shouldn't seem rehearsed."

It didn't, thanks to Eddie Vos, who was not going to let anything
as minor as a movie interfere with his routine. Just when Cosgrove
had the lighting perfect, Petrik, state-of-the-art camera slung over
his shoulder, twisted into a properly grotesque caricature, was
ready to film, Grimm with a smile, saying he had a fistful of aces,
about to bet, audience poised for a vintage Bobby Blanco performance (he had a heart flush), Harris about to say "Take one," just
when all this drama was about to be captured for posterity, Eddie
Vos decided to clean his red-hot grill with a pail of water.

In seconds the galley filled with smoke. Spiess led the charge
out to the deck. Everyone inhaled gulps of ocean air, and tried to
avoid going overboard. Of those in the galley, only Eddie maintained his post. He emerged about ten minutes later to say
everything was normal and to ask what was the fuss about. Troop-
ing back to the interrupted movie site, Grimm was observed
carrying the poker hand he held when the game was stopped.

"Don't bet that heart flush, Bobby."

"In five-card draw?"

"I think Grimm has four of a kind."

"Do you know what the odds are against that?"

"Odds don't apply to this character."

The movie portrayed accurately. Every set of eyes bored into
Grimm to see which side of the deck the cards came from, but his
seeming world-record winning streak went on nonetheless. Lowenstein was asked once again to compute the probabilities, but he
wouldn't involve himself.

Work was impossible with the heavy sea, so the game ground
on. Spiess more regularly stopped to observe its progress.

The tycoon's demeanor never varied: shy and humble. He was embarrassed by his unprecedented "run of luck," generous with compliments for his opponents' brand of play, always certain a change of tide lurked just around the corner. But, he never failed to rake in a pot. The sea didn't spill *his* chips onto the floor, and as careful as Scrooge's bookkeeper he kept the IOUs current. He professed to miss Bobby's outbursts—the Cuban's fire was temporarily put out—and tortured his victims by stopping critical hands in mid-deal to exchange off-color jokes with Captain Armand. He seemed to be blessed with never-ending luck. His biggest gamble, however, was yet to come.

On July 8 we were one day from Titanic Canyon, and finally set to begin the *Titanic* search.

First thing in the morning, Fred Spiess held a meeting to kick off officially this most important portion of the trip. Spiess said a few words and then introduced Bill Ryan, who, of course, everyone knew by now. The Lamont-Doherty oceanographer talked about the geological features we would encounter, then turned the meeting back to Spiess, who introduced Jack Grimm. Grimm delivered a pep talk. Then, being the gambler that he is, he asked everyone to guess where the *Titanic* would be found. It was almost an informal lottery, so everyone, as if we were not interested enough, would have a rooting interest.

Spiess chose the Number One target, which was the acoustic shadow indicating a feature of more than eighty feet in height, and a length of nine hundred feet. But then he fudged his answer, perhaps because of some unwritten law faithfully adhered to by scientists, that one *never* guesses, even if the purpose is merely good fun.

"I've got no favorites," said Ryan, really hedging.

"I think it's Number Thirteen," said Mark Olsson, a Scripps scientist catching the spirit of the occasion. Thirteen was the linear reflective object nine hundred to a thousand feet in length that cast a clear, large shadow close in shape to what could be expected from the *Titanic's* hull.

John Jain said he wouldn't make a choice, but got into the spirit and went with Number One. So did Wayne Wardlow, Captain Armand, Jim Drury, and I.

"I'll take Number Ten," and Bobby Blanco. This was the "little banana," three reflective objects that cast shadows along the wall of Titanic Canyon.

Scripps scientist Mary Linzer chose Number Seven, a broad reflective patch measuring eight hundred by two hundred fifty feet. Anita Brosius said Number Thirteen, siding with Mark Olsson. Nik Petrik said Number Ten.

Grimm was the most precise of all. "It's Number One," he contended, "or it's a mile west of Number One."

Before the meeting broke up, Grimm laughed and announced he really was conducting a lottery. A map of the search area had been drawn, and cordoned into numerous squares. Each person aboard the *Gyre* was assigned a square, and the person occupying the one containing the *Titanic* won two round-trip tickets to Las Vegas and an all-expense-paid weekend. A number of us, painfully aware of his terrific luck in our evening poker games, felt sure he would win his own lottery.

For Harris and Grimm reaching the search site was the culmination of years of planning and organizing. But everyone else was keyed up too.

The monotony of HEBBLE was forgotten. People even looked forward to watch duty. As a steady rain had become a hard downpour, Cosgrove, reading another Western novel in his bunk, seemed a good role model to emulate. We had some days ahead, and a relaxing book seemed in order.

Only the books were filled with reminiscences of those who had been there, and were not exactly "relaxing." One occupant of a life boat recalled,

The captainstoker told us that he had been at sea twenty-six years, and had never yet seen such a calm night on the Atlantic. As we rowed away from the *Titanic*, we looked back from time to time to watch her and a more striking spectacle it was not possible for anyone to see. In the distance it looked an enormous length, its great bulk outlined in black against the starry sky, every porthole and saloon blazing with light.

Johanna Stunke, a passenger aboard the *Bremen,* later saw many of the dead in the water. Her account lent credence to Grimm's belief that following the trail of bodies would lead us back to the *Titanic*.

It was between four and five o'clock, Saturday April 20, Mrs. Stunke recalled,

> when our ship sighted an iceberg off the bow to the starboard. As we drew nearer, and could make out small dots floating around in the sea, a feeling of awe and sadness crept over everyone on the ship.
>
> We passed within a hundred feet of the southernmost drift of the wreckage, and looking down over the rail we distinctly saw a number of bodies so clearly that we could make out what they were wearing and whether they were men or women.
>
> We saw one woman in her night dress, with a baby clasped closely to her breast. Several women passengers screamed and left the rail in a fainting condition. There was another woman, fully dressed, with her arms tight around the body of a shaggy dog.
>
> The bodies of three men in a group, all clinging to one steamship chair, floated nearby, and just beyond them were a dozen bodies of men, all of them encased in life preservers clinging together as though in a last desperate struggle for life.

The *Bremen* did not pick up the bodies, because the White Star Line's *Mackay Bennett* had been specifically sent to perform the task, and was only two hours away. The *Mackay Bennett* carried one hundred ninety bodies to Halifax, and one hundred thirteen more were buried at sea.

Seventeen enginemen perished aboard the *Titanic*, but their heroism saved numerous lives. By putting out fires flaring in the boilers, rather than seeking safety, they gained a precious extra hour for the *Titanic* to disembark passengers.

I spent most of the afternoon and the entire evening reading the melancholy material. The only break was for dinner, which was sandwiches. Cook Eddie Vos was not losing his touch; it was just that the sea was so rough, and the galley pitching so violently, that food that required dishes was likely to find its way to the floor or the ceiling.

"Well, Cosgrove," I said just before turning out the light, "tomorrow's the day."

"I hope we find her right away," he said. "I hate suspense."

By the 8 A.M. winch-watch the next morning all but one of the transponders, those key navigating tools, were down. Bill Ryan, still declining to specify where, predicted we would find the *Titanic* "in three or four days."

A forty-knot wind blew, hardly conducive to finding anything. Ever since the voyage had begun, reports had reached us of ships in trouble and people going overboard. More than once Captain Armand had been on the verge of turning the *Gyre* and hurrying to assist another vessel. The sea had a way of reminding us she was not to be trifled with nor would she surrender her secrets easily.

Only a few months later, in February, 1982, the North Atlantic would demonstrate once again her contempt for the efforts and inventions of mere people. A couple of hundred miles from where we looked, the world's biggest oil rig, Mobil Oil's *Ocean Ranger*, capsized and all eighty-four people working aboard were killed; just thirty-six hours after that, the Russian freighter *Mekhanik Tarasov* went down in the same area, losing thirty-six.

It was treacherous everywhere on the *Gyre* but especially on deck. Outside stairways resembled miniature Niagara Falls, water cascaded down them in powerful rushes, while the main danger inside was falling and cracking your head.

Our electronic "fish" didn't go into the water until 4:30 that afternoon. Again the hardy band of scientists, with the film crew recording their moves, seemed certain to be separated from our tiny ship. Somehow, they all managed to hang on, and the fish was successfully launched in the storm.

People now *wanted* to be on watch, particularly in the lab where it was expected that the *Titanic*'s discovery would first be confirmed. No longer was Spiess and his magnetometer reading, Lowenstein and his friend the computer, and navigator Farre the objects of nonscientific derision. Their every move was studied. No one would find the *Titanic* if they didn't.

At 11:30 that evening, the "fish," a half mile behind the *Gyre* and two-and-a-half miles down, was towed forty-three fathoms from the ocean bottom over the first of our targets, Number Six. In 1980 Six had been sonified on three separate runs, and on one of these a clear shadow was cast. It was considered a top priority, although no one had chosen it in the lounge the day before.

The lab's sensitive equipment registered nothing as the "fish" passed over the site. *Nothing*.

"How could it be nothing?" Bobby Blanco was asked. "Surely it was *something*." Then he shrugged his shoulders. He had been out the year before, learning to take disappointment in stride. Also, he had not believed it would be Six, he had chosen Ten, and so his disappointment was not too great.

Bobby was right in one way of thinking. We had fourteen targets, and the *Titanic* could only be in one of them.

"Maybe we went over the wrong spot."

"Not much chance of that. These guys can get you where you want to go."

Thirteen was next, the linear reflective object nine hundred to one thousand feet in length that cast the *Titanic*-size shadow. Mark Olsson had chosen this target, and indeed it seemed to be one of our main hopes. Grimm had called it odds-on before further thought changed his opinion.

We would pass over Thirteen at 1:15 A.M., and fifteen minutes before the event the lab was packed. Captain Armand came to watch; his desire to find the ship was among the strongest.

The first and most critical sign of success would register on the "maggie," the magnetometer that picked up the presence of metal. We would run the camera equipment down and photograph the great ship if the magnetometer lines bounced crazily, as everyone hoped they would.

Time dragged. The lab was cramped, close, uncomfortable. "We over it yet, Farre?"

No answer.

"Let us know when we're over it, Farre."

"Take it easy," said Bobby.

Again, nothing registered. How was *this* possible? Here was an object picked up on sonar the year before that was the length of the *Titanic*.

"We passed it on the wrong side," said Farre. "We'll pick it up coming back."

"That sea is murder," said Bobby. "Almost impossible going to a precise spot in weather like this. At least Thirteen's not ruled out. We'll come back to it."

But the disappointment was clearly visible on many faces. Hopes had been held out for Six and Thirteen, and next on the agenda was Number Seven, which nobody really believed in: this was the broad reflective patch at the base of the south wall of Titanic Canyon, measuring eight hundred by two hundred fifty feet.

"Best to get some sleep," said Bobby. "Number One comes after Number Seven, and we'll want to be awake for it."

The lab, except for the scheduled watch crew, emptied quickly. No one wanted to miss Number One.

As luck would have it, most people did miss the passage over Number One, at least the nonscientific ones, because it was not clear how quickly events were going to happen. HEBBLE, slower than snails, had lulled us to a false pace, but now things would move, one important event crowding in upon another.

At 5:30 A.M. it was too late to be in the lab for the passage over Number One, that acoustic shadow eighty feet high, nine hundred feet long picked by so many as emanating from the *Titanic*. We had already gone over it, and over Number Seven. The blip that registered on the magnetometer was like a dead man's heartbeat.

"We did pick up something at Number One," said Ryan.

"You did? Great. What?"

"We think it's geology," said Ryan. This meant he believed it was a natural metal formation which would affect the magnetometer just as something man-made would. "But we'll make another pass over the target."

Previously there had been an easy camaraderie, everybody aboard the *Gyre* seemed genuinely to like one another, but the atmosphere was different this early morning.

Tony Boegeman's face was hard. Lowenstein, the self-styled deep thought, had a faraway expression, and even the gregarious Drury had fewer good things than usual to say about his fellow passengers.

Each person reacted differently. Bobby Blanco, our resident pessimist, mentioned something about scientists acquiring equipment on false premises. Nik Petrik was philosophical, talking about déjà vu and remembering the previous year's trip that began with such high hopes and suffered disappointment on top of disappointment. Grimm, almost a cheerleader two mornings before in the lounge, was afflicted by fatalism: "What you really want," he said, "never comes easy. Sometimes it never comes at all." But we had gone over fewer than half of our targets and were returning to two of the more probable; this search had just begun. Yet there seemed to be a certain fatalism in the air, as if we were all, as one, steeling ourselves for failure.

Being alone on the winch-watch was a relief after the oppressive atmosphere inside. It was gray, rough, and unpleasant, but preferable to everyone snapping at one another and witnessing the loss of good-naturedness, which seemed certain to accelerate.

We went back over Number One, and the scientists declared it definitely not the *Titanic*. At 11:20 A.M. Farre reported "a magnetic anomaly that's interesting" discovered as we towed from Number One to Number Thirteen.

"When Spiess gets up," Farre said, "he'll look at it, and see if it deserves further checking."

Spiess was awake shortly, declared himself unimpressed, and said it was a waste of time to go back to the anomaly: much too small for anything as large as the *Titanic*.

This was the part of the expedition the movie crew was on hand to film, and they were all over the ship, doing their best, but realizing that most of it was for naught if we didn't find the *Titanic*.

Drury, the on-camera narrator, enjoyed locating himself in dangerous positions before delivering his lines. He probably thought that waves crashing over his head as he talked provided a you-are-there atmosphere, and his favorite positions were slipping and sliding on the bow, hanging precariously on to the railing of the fantail, and getting soaked on the winch-watch, during particularly heavy rainstorms. Once he perched himself atop the winch itself, a groaning, squeaking monster playing out heavy steel cable, and talked about how hazardous it was for the scientists.

At about three that afternoon the lab again filled, this time for a second pass over Thirteen, the linear reflective object that cast the *Titanic*-size shadow. Hopes were high here, the number of people on hand to observe being the giveaway. Grimm, crammed up against the hefty Burris, looked like a man who feared being crushed. Since it was impossible to see the instruments the scientists were reading through the crush of people (if they could have been seen, it would have been almost as difficult to tell what information they provided—impossible in the case of Lowenstein's computer gear), the best bet was to try to read their faces for traces of good news. Was Spiess smiling? Was that a flicker in his eyes? Did Lowenstein leaning back slightly mean his computer was relaying something encouraging? Or was it a gesture of disappointment? Or did his back just hurt? What did Boegeman's grunt convey? Of course, not one of them would *say* what was going on.

"Congratulations," said Farre to Gleason, who was guiding the ship, "you've just eliminated another target." Though he was trying to be funny, Farre felt as bad as anyone that another target was scratched.

When we earlier went past Number Six, nothing registered, but now Lowenstein, seemingly never off the job, always in his little niche in the back of the lab, discovered that his computer, outdoing the maggie, had found a trace of anomalies at Six. Spiess ordered another pass over Six and if that failed we would head for Number Ten: Bobby's choice, "the little banana," a curled slump feature containing three reflective objects that cast shadows along the wall of Titanic Canyon.

We went over Number Six at about 7:30 P.M., and the consensus held it wasn't the *Titanic*. The magnetometer just didn't register anything. Why, then, had Lowenstein's computer? For this reason Number Six could not completely be ruled out.

On the way to Number Ten there was time to talk, about anything and everything. Drury talked about entering a hang-gliding competition on Grimm's mountain outside Abilene, though he had never tried the sport. John Farre revealed a little about himself, including an adventure of being trapped in a nuclear submarine on the bottom of the ocean and another time briefly being a Son of Sam suspect. He had turned two spent bullets he had found over to the police during the hunt for the .22 calibre killer. Though an act of civic responsibility, it had caused him to be investigated. The events of the last hours, or lack of them, had made people a little giddy and garrulous.

On the way to Number Ten, Bill Ryan had a worried look on his face. He was asked what was wrong.

"After Ten," said Ryan, "they push me overboard."

"Why's that?"

"All the high priorities will be gone."

"Then it has to be Ten."

But it wasn't. The magnetometer needle stayed as still as death. It took all of Bobby's sense of irony and humor to say: "We're down to Grimm's luck now. We let him fly the 'fish' and hope he crashes it into the *Titanic*."

Ryan, unlike Spiess, was more open with his emotions. No one watching him could doubt how much he wanted to find the ship. He disappeared after the pass over Number Ten and wasn't spotted until much later, sitting alone with his chin in his hands in a darkened anteroom off the deserted lounge.

Spiess was different. He probably would have looked the same if the "fish" had just hooked the *Titanic* and pulled it to the top. He said we would make another run over Number Ten, and the *Gyre* began the tedious process of turning in the water.

The movie crew was busy through most of this. Grimm's film would not go unused. When Drury wasn't conducting interviews or taking chances on some uncertain perch, Harris, Cosgrove, Petrik, and Bobby captured every element of the expedition, the physical, purely muscle part, as well as the scientific.

If Grimm was defeated, and some said he was, it didn't show. The most obvious difference in the millionaire's manner was interest, not previously evident, in the smallest scientific details. His background in geology qualified him as a scientist, and the way Spiess, Ryan, and he now talked, he clearly understood what was happening.

"What do you think is the problem?" Petrik was asked.

"A massive case of the dumbs," he said. "We believe we know more than we do."

"You think it's hopeless?"

"I didn't say that. But I don't like what I see coming. It was the same last year."

"What's coming?"

"The scientists are already talking about 'the other guys,' meaning us, being responsible. If only they hadn't been distracted by a circus, if only more technocrats instead of writers and cameramen and actors had been brought, if only blah blah blah. And they'll blame each other when they get tired of this. The Scripps people will blame the Lamont people, and vice versa."

Eddie Vos made some sense. "The *Titanic's* big," he said. "But the ocean's bigger."

"Big, dark, and deep," added Jack Cosgrove.

The magnetometer, upon which so much hope was placed, "saw" 1,200 feet on each side, 2,400 feet in all. What the maggie was mostly doing was systematically eliminating one 1980 sonar target after another.

At 1:25 A.M. we passed over Number Ten again. This time we obtained a sonar image, a shadow, but the magnetometer registered a disappointing nothing. Number Ten couldn't be eliminated, but it was a longshot.

The galley at 4:30 the next morning looked as it might at noon. Not many could sleep. Spiess, trying to lighten the mood, said it wasn't our fault, his wife had predicted failure, claiming the Russians had already come and taken the *Titanic* away.

At 6 A.M. on the way from Number Ten to Number Eleven, a

magnetic anomaly was detected. It was large enough to guarantee we would come back to check. When discoveries such as this occurred, it just wasn't possible to turn back immediately: The *Gyre*, towing the heavy "fish," required hours to turn around and steam in the opposite direction.

Nothing was found at Eleven, so it was off to Number Twelve. Bobby Blanco said he could not recall ever having felt so discouraged. "We'll find her at Number Twelve," said John Farre, his voice so filled with authority that he was almost believable.

We didn't find the *Titanic* at Twelve, and eliminated the anomaly when it was revisited. In all we were combing an area of approximately thirty square miles, but distance in the empty Atlantic was impossible to judge with the naked eye. To follow our course it was necessary to look at the lines on a grid as we crossed and crisscrossed the area where the targets had been located.

There was always hope as we approached a target, then a silent wait for the next target.

Number Five was next, and on the way to it another anomaly was found. The discovery of metal always elicited a surge of optimism, even among some of the younger scientists, who had begun to share the belief that if we discovered the *Titanic* it would be largely by luck. Everyone was sure that the thirty-square-mile area put us in the ballpark; we might stumble over her.

With each failure people tried harder. Lowenstein, the chair, and the computer melded into one. If Spiess slept, no one saw him. And no one complained about watch duty anymore. Ryan and Anita Brosius worked on Lamont-Doherty's "fish" (the one in the water belonged to Scripps) in case it was called on to substitute. The feature of the Lamont "fish" was its color television equipment, but there seemed no hope it would go into the water unless we found something. Still, Ryan and Anita slept almost as little as the tireless Spiess. Trying harder, an undefinable will seemed all we had left.

Spiess stayed up all night calculating the anomalies we had

registered just in the various passages we had made across Titanic Canyon. The magnetometer had registered fifty tons of anomalies. That was the good news. The bad news was the anomalies were scattered; if they represented the *Titanic*, the ship was broken up.

"I wish there were just one," said Tony Boegeman.

This mood prevailed among most people aboard, but not Grimm. His attitude was the most healthy of all, for he was interested in finding out whatever her fate had been. As John Jain said, something very peculiar was in Titanic Canyon. Maybe a fortune in ore.

For the first time since HEBBLE the weather was beautiful. At Mike Harris's suggestion the movie crew and assorted others decided it was a good time to go out in a *Zodiac*, the boat made famous by Jacques Cousteau, to do underwater filming. They donned their wet suits, scuba gear, flippers, all the accoutrements necessary for deep-sea diving. A missing part of the plan was someone who knew how to pilot the boat.

"I'll do it," volunteered engine room helper John Burris.

No one else volunteered. Mark Olsson, a professional lifeguard and expert scuba diver, saw Burris didn't know how to get into the *Zodiac* and started to offer advice. He was in the process of explaining that when the tide was carrying the *Zodiac* up was the time to jump, not to jump when the boat was going down, but before he could finish Burris's three hundred pounds were over the rail. His timing was off, and the *Zodiac* came close to going two and a half miles down.

He got the engine going and the large canoe-type vessel zipped across the ocean, stopping rabbitlike fifty yards from the *Gyre*.

Anita and Bobby, the most professional, slipped backward over the *Zodiac* into the sea. Anita was too close to the motor's whirling blades and in danger of having her legs sliced off. Burris reacted by gunning the *Zodiac* in a crazed circle, just barely missing her.

Simultaneous with the *Zodiac* drama was another involving Jack Cosgrove. He had dived off the fantail to get shots from a different angle, and he flailed for a moment and went stiff in the water. Bobby Blanco sized it up at once. With a powerful stroke he went after Cosgrove, forty yards away, mowing through the water. The ocean was too cold, and the shock afflicting the cameraman would lead to drowning if human help didn't arrive right away.

Spiess was livid. He was unapproachable. Amateurs had been out and saying something wasn't worth it. It was impossible for anyone seeing Cosgrove stiff in the water, Anita vulnerable with Burris steering, Bobby swimming powerfully through the waves, to forget how close it had been.

The mood on board ship was already tense, and these two fiascos served to heighten it. Everyone blamed everyone else. Captain Armand who, had he known about it, would have stopped anyone going out, summed it up best: "Without directions, some people on this ship couldn't pour piss out of a boot."

Panic began to creep in. Grimm advocated replacing the Scripps "fish" with the Lamont-Doherty one, equipped with color-camera equipment. He wanted pictures. If we couldn't find the ship we could stun a movie audience with film depicting life at world record depths; the search would not be a total failure.

John Farre spoke up against the failing attitude. He argued, at considerable risk to himself (his boss, Ryan, was dying to put *his* "fish" in the water), that we should go on with the Scripps Deep Tow; we weren't defeated at all.

A practical consideration ended the debate. A part on the drive shaft that drove the winch broke. Nothing was possible without the winch feeding the crane that fed the "fish." The search was over.

Grimm, as usual, cut through the red tape and radioed the later-to-be-doomed *Ocean Ranger* and asked if he could use their machine shop to repair the part. Of course, they answered. Brother Grimm was in trouble, and, sure, *Ocean Ranger* would help.

But *Ocean Ranger* was two hundred miles away, far off our

course, and Grimm searched for another idea. He radioed La-mont-Doherty. Do you have a replacement part? Indeed they did.

They arranged to fly the part from New Jersey to St. John's, and then for a small plane to rendezvous with us two hundred miles off the coast and parachute the part down to the *Gyre*. The operation would cost us three days, but was quicker than using *Ocean Ranger*'s machine shop.

"I think I can fix the part," said Mark Olsson. It seemed impossible, for the piece had to be ground to a fineness of one thousandth of an inch, but Grimm told him to go ahead and try. The remarkable Olssson disappeared into a cubbyhole off the engine room and the *Gyre* steamed toward St. John's.

What in hell were we doing out here, pampering a millionaire's whim, away from our families; all the luxuries in the world didn't make it pleasant, and it was tempting to try to swim back.

How low could morale sink? News arrived that the plane carrying the part was fogged in at Newark. Worse, even if it reached St. John's, it would be fogged in there.

"We're in big trouble, boys," Grimm was told.

The millionaire didn't think it was funny.

When all hope was abandoned, the seemingly impossible happened. Olsson fixed the part. We were back in business, but why? We had eliminated the targets, and we had failed to find the *Titanic*.

A high-level meeting was held (only Grimm, Spiess, and Ryan were included), and the decision was made to expand the search area. Grimm had paid for time for the *Gyre* and he was manic about finding the *Titanic*, and we weren't going to quit.

Out on the winch-watch the wind blew hard, but warm. We searched the ocean wildly (but the grids made sense; on these you could see the crisscross logic of the oceanographers). Maybe logic wouldn't solve this riddle, and maybe bad weather would ensure our failure.

The *Gyre* just wasn't big enough to function effectively in rough water. Ryan pointed out that all kinds of future useful benefits were possible because of what we had learned. As time was running out the future was not what Grimm wanted to hear about.

We looked at photographs taken during a long run through Titanic Canyon. We saw what appeared to be an air duct, a cannon barrel, a piece of pipe, and another piece of metal the size and shape of a king-sized bed that had a hole in the middle. Grimm judged this debris "was probably from the *Titanic*."

We had use of the ship for only one more day. It had next been chartered to the U.S. Geological Survey and was required back in Boston.

This was unacceptable to Grimm. A flurry of radio calls, wheedling, wheeling-dealing, pleas, threats, reason, emotion, resulted in a one-day extension. The U.S. Geological Survey would give us one more day.

The big finale—and it was a good one—featured Grimm, Ryan, and Spiess. It was a meeting long anticipated, and the millionaire laid down the law. We had one day left, and at least we were going to have good pictures of the ocean floor. Grimm wanted Spiess to pull his "fish" out of the water and Ryan to put his in. We'd make one long last run down Titanic Canyon; Ryan's television camera recording it all, and we'd at least have footage for the movie.

There were fifty tons of anomalies down there and he wanted to *see* what they were; the magnetometer was getting us nowhere. It was one final gamble by a man who had gambled himself out of an Oklahoma backwater to an enormous amount of money and wasn't accustomed to failing.

Spiess didn't like it. He said the Scripps Deep Tow offered our best hope. Everyone had agreed on that at the start, and it was a mistake to go to the Lamont fish. But he was overruled.

Ryan was ecstatic. His equipment would be put to the test. If his fish didn't find the *Titanic*, he would be in illustrious company.

Of course, the television apparatus he had built from scratch might not function, but it was a risk worth taking.

The Lamont-Doherty fish replaced the Scripps Deep Tow equipment. We towed the canyon taking movie footage until our deadline ran out. The hour came and went when we had to stop and turn around to head for Boston.

Grimm resembled a man at his own execution, pleading for "just one more day," then one hour, and finally "how about thirty minutes?" He got the extra thirty minutes. His by-now legendary good fortune was about to assert itself.

"*The sea never changes and its works, for all the talk of men, are wrapped in mystery.*"

—Joseph Conrad,
The Typhoon

BEYOND REACH

Not even Ryan had known if his color television equipment would work. If it did, it was believed he would have set a world record. Probably no one had ever taken television pictures at such a depth.

It was 10 P.M., and a big crowd gathered in the lounge. "The last hurrah," said Nik Petrik. The *Gyre* was no longer searching for the *Titanic* but was headed to Boston. What followed was an utterly engrossing three-hour television production, featuring pictures no human could have seen before. It was dark in the lounge and so crowded people had to be warned not to get too close to the set. The only understandable words were congratulations being thrown at Bill Ryan. The Lamont scientist tried and failed to conceal his pride, but insisted the accomplishment was shared by Anita Brosius, John Farre, and Dale Chayes.

We saw a shrimp at least a foot long, a species of fish the scientists had not known existed, a starfish as large as a motorcycle wheel, as well as things that looked like a coffin, George Washington's skull, an old bottle, and a tin cup.

Some of the strange fish that swam into view mugged for the camera, although the silent Lamont "fish" must have been as strange to them as they to us.

We were into the last thirty minutes, the extra half-hour that Grimm had wheedled from the U.S. Geological Survey. No one transfixed by that television was prepared for what was coming.

It appeared all of a sudden, out of nowhere, and a simultaneous gasp erupted from all of us. It was so huge and unexpected it took our breath away.

Grimm came off his chair as if propelled by a cannon. He said right off it was a propeller from the *Titanic* and ordered the tape played back. Replay it we did. Endlessly. The tycoon couldn't get enough of it. It was always dramatic. From a sea empty of life, just rushing water, stunningly it was *there*. It looked to be the twenty-six tons a *Titanic* propeller would weigh. The television footage was so impressive because what was captured appeared suddenly, a colossus right before the eyes, and then it was gone.

What had John Jain been thinking? Of course it would happen this way—not slowly, dreamlike—given the speed at which the "fish" was being towed.

Everyone had the sense of something awesome being encountered, but Ryan would not concede it was the *Titanic's* propeller. He risked being laughed at by colleagues if he made such a judgment from television footage alone. But in his bones Grimm knew he had passed over the great ship which obsessed him. He called on Captain Armand, who had not watched the unprecedented footage, to take a look. No one was to say anything to Armand. He would be shown the film and asked what it was.

"It's a propeller," he said without reservation.

"From the *Titanic*?" Grimm asked.

"It's consistent in size."

The millionaire was off in a rush to the radio room. He had

risked a fortune to find the legendary ship—she was found he felt—how could anyone be so shortsighted not to give him more time now?

The government could. Grimm had already wangled an extra day; there would be no more. The millionaire turned on the charm, resorted to reason, threw in a few heavyweight names who were friends, and hinted he had political clout. Then he begged, imitating (I think he was imitating) a man on the verge of tears. He harangued and wouldn't stop complaining even after it was obvious the cause was hopeless. The bureaucracy was not going to budge.

What Grimm wanted was to turn the *Gyre* around and go back and photograph the entire ship. What could be more important? "Probably they've got another HEBBLE planned," he raged, "and nuts to something people really care about: What happened to the *Titanic*."

We closed in on Boston in the next few days. Five hundred miles out Farre said he could smell the city, which obliged Nik Petrik to say the only smell was Farre's unwashed laundry.

Lots of dolphins played and whales blew water as we drew near home, relaxation, and revival guaranteed by just watching them. The sun was warm and protective; nothing like in that godforsaken area where the *Titanic* went down.

Despite Grimm's failure to win us an extension, the return voyage to Boston was enjoyable. Grimm seemed to be plotting how to wrest control of the *Gyre* from Captain Armand's hands and return to the *Titanic*, but the rest of us were letting down from the excitement and anticipation. Promises to stay in touch and visit after we went separate ways were exchanged.

The dramatic television footage provided by the Lamont scientists was the subject of endless discussion. Yet it was evident that what was needed was a painstaking analysis in the serenity of a lab, not in a hectic late-night scenario in a lounge with a millionaire trying to turn a U.S. Navy ship around.

It is the nature of children—natural naifs, not yet schooled in the ways of "seeing"—to point out what truly is before our eyes. Adults have their own peculiar prejudices that limit them. Children, unencumbered by decades of layering their superegos, see clearly.

I once heard a story about a child and his father riding in the observation car of a train traveling across Arizona and New Mexico bound for Los Angeles.

The boy was precocious, studying the terrain he saw shimmering outside, alternately amazed and bored. He asked his father an endless series of questions. One of them was, "When will we get to Arizona?"

His father did his best to explain that except in the case of a natural boundary like a body of water borders are man's way of drawing lines. The boy may or may not have understood his father's explanation, but he surely would have been far happier if someone had applied a thick, black line through the desert to delineate which state was which.

To people young or old, compartmentalization is nearly always a good, unspoken, sometimes unconscious tool we use to make the world conform.

That may be why many who have written of the *Titanic* saw its foundering as a turning point. The arguments run like this: the Victorian Age, the Golden Age (or as Mark Twain scoffed, the Gilded Age), preached a Calvinistic pursuit of worldly goods. Burgeoning technology allowed more people to accumulate the accoutrements of a comfortable life. Thus, according to many writers on the subject, that ultimately shattered the world as it had been known.

Perhaps the horrible screams that were heard to echo over the North Atlantic that April 15 embody a symbol. Not many months later the world went to war, and that war was fought with modern weaponry unlike any the world had seen—flying machines, mustard gas, and other new unprecedented weapons and systems to deliver them. The numbing shock of the unsinkable ship sinking like a stone set off a sequence of changes. Probably few minds had viewed "the night to remember" as an epiphany that called to a halt the juggernaut of progress as it had up until then been perceived. The message was heard, the rules were changed (no more sea lanes in the northern extremes of the Atlantic during iceberg season). But progress goes on, and man's confidence, while shaken, recovers.

The world got on with its business after the events of April 1912, but not quite as if nothing had happened. The survivors had the strongest responses to it all, of course, and their reactions many years after are instructive. Some lived on many decades. More than one writer who chronicled the *Titanic*'s tale has pointed out that they are a vigorous lot.

Like Gus Cohen, known as The Cat for his remarkable ability to survive disasters. He survived the *Titanic* sinking, a head wound in World War I, a bombing in World War II, and being struck by a car while riding a bicycle in the 1960s.

To others who survived the sinking, after they had outlived their nightmares, the simple fact of their survival was an incentive to live life fully. To experience an event of the enormity of the one they lived through instilled a belief, perhaps conscious, in what Albert Schweitzer called "reverence for life." Loosely translated from the German, the notion is perhaps best paraphrased as a fear before an overwhelming force. As one of Schweitzer's biographers has put it, "reverence for life" reverberates with " . . . the feelings we experience on the tops of high mountains, in a storm at sea, or in a tropical tornado . . . an acknowledgment of the immensity and of the vastness of nature." It also implies a new strength born of the recognition.

That the sinking was a tragedy can be argued. The event had its heroes, including Captain Smith, a man of strength and courage who, through a tragic weakness, obeyed his masters instead of his common sense and drove his ship into the iceberg. There is a wonderful mise-en-scène along with the other accoutrements of Aristotelian tragedy. But that argument is academic. After all is said, the sinking was not tragic so much as it was dumb.

The event is most extraordinary not because of any intrinsic dramatic merit but because of the response. The blow delivered to the world's consciousness compares to only one event in recent decades: the assassination of President Kennedy. The events are vastly different in scope. But, if within the lifetimes of people who can remember both events, science comes to understand the brain well enough to examine memory tissues, those minute bits that store the two events will, I think, bear a terrible similarity.

Mankind is rarely moved as one consciousness. The impact of the two events shared that profound power. And both events have been adopted as moments of demarcation in history.

When Grimm got back to Abilene he found a picture sent to him from England. The photo was of a propeller salvaged from the *Oceanic*, which went down in 1918. The two ships had very similar propellers and looking at the two they seemed identical.

The television pictures were studied until eyeballs almost fell out. Most noteworthy was the realization that our propeller seemed to hang in the water above the ocean floor. Unless basic physical laws were violated, this meant it was attached to the shaft that, it seemed, was attached to the ship.

One of Ryan's objections was we had found the propeller outside the search area. Here Grimm made a real contribution to *Titanic* lore. Hardly an avid reader, he had nonetheless pored through *Titanic* literature and discovered what had gone unnoticed. The *Titanic*'s radio operator had given the wrong distress position, because the ship's clock had not been moved back twenty minutes as was required every four hours. Taking this understandable error into consideration, the propeller was exactly where it ought to have been.

In San Antonio Jim Drury gave a speech to the elite Explorers

Club. When he showed pictures of what Grimm found, all agreed it was a propeller.

"I found her, boy," Grimm said over the telephone.

"You probably did, Jack."

"I'm going back next year," said the driven man. "Right back to where we shot the propeller. We'll get the whole show this time."

I believe him. And I also think, in some not quite reasoning part of my brain, that Thomas Andrews is, at least in spirit, waiting at the other end of that propeller shaft. Perhaps he is urging on Jack Grimm and his obsession with finding the *Titanic*. Somehow, however, I think not. Thomas Andrews, builder of the ship beyond reach, wants it that way for now.

APPENDIX

TITANIC HISTORICAL SOCIETY

1982 ANNUAL MEETING AND PRESS CONFERENCE

LIVING TITANIC SURVIVOR STATEMENTS

JACK GRIMM, Speaker:
We are visiting with Mrs. Ruth Blanchard, one of the survivors of the *Titanic*. We are in the Maritime Museum in Philadelphia, and this is the seventieth anniversary of the sinking of the *Titanic*. Welcome to Philadelphia, Mrs. Blanchard.

MRS. BLANCHARD: Thank you very much.

JACK GRIMM: Will you tell us a little bit about what class you were on and at what point in time were you told that the *Titanic* was going to sink and to get your life preservers on? Now we understand that some of the survivors in steerage class were not told until the last minute, and by that time all the lifeboats were gone. What was your experience?

MRS. BLANCHARD: Well, we were in bed and my mother noticed that the engines had stopped in mid-ocean and she was worried. People were running around the halls and upstairs, so she went and poked her head out the door and asked a steward out there. And he said there wasn't too much the matter. They were going to go on in a few minutes. So she came back to bed and we laid there for ten or fifteen minutes and she got nervous. She decided to put on her robe and she went out and met the cabin steward and he said, "Put on your things and come at once." She said, "Do we have time to dress?" and he said, "No madam. You have time for nothing. Put on your life belts and your clothes, shoes, and stockings and come up to the top deck." So that is what we did. We put the shoes and stockings on and dressed my little brother and sister. We didn't dress ourselves. And we didn't put any life belts on. Then we went up to the top deck and closed deck to wait for orders.

JACK GRIMM: And how many members of your family were evacuated from the ship?

MRS. BLANCHARD: Well, my mother and my little brother who was two years old and my sister, who was four years old. I was twelve.

JACK GRIMM: And your father was not on board?

MRS. BLANCHARD: No, he had to stay back in India and work another year before he came to America.

JACK GRIMM: And you all boarded the same lifeboat?

MRS. BLANCHARD: No, we didn't. My brother and sister and my mother were on one lifeboat and I was on another because they didn't have room. First they were going to take the little ones and they wouldn't let my mother on and she screamed and said, "Please let me on, those are my children." Then I was left and she said, "Try and get on another boat." So I did.

JACK GRIMM: You were very courageous to get in the other boat.

MRS. BLANCHARD: Well, I didn't think for a minute but that I could get on another boat, and I would see her later, you see.

JACK GRIMM: Oh, yes.

MRS. BLANCHARD: I don't know why, but that's what I thought.

JACK GRIMM: Were most of the lifeboats congregated in one

central area when the *Carpathia* came to pick you up or were they scattered?

MRS. BLANCHARD: They were scattered.

JACK GRIMM: And was the wind blowing? Do you have any knowledge whether the wind was from the north, and were the lifeboats drifting in a southerly direction?

MRS. BLANCHARD: I don't know anything about that, except that I do know that it was very very calm when we got off, just like a mill pond. But toward morning, the waves got rough and we just bounced around like a little cork.

JACK GRIMM: We searched for the *Titanic* the last two summers, of 1980 and 1981, and last summer we found what we believe to be one of the propellers of the *Titanic*. We found it halfway between where the *Titanic's* corrected S.O.S. position was and where the lifeboats were found.

MRS. BLANCHARD: Oh, I see.

JACK GRIMM: So we are curious as to how much movement and how far the lifeboats drifted before the *Carpathia* arrived. Did you have the feeling that the boat was drifting?

MRS. BLANCHARD: I didn't have any idea about that.

JACK GRIMM: Was anyone rowing?

MRS. BLANCHARD: Yes.

JACK GRIMM: You were rowing, but you weren't sure in what direction?

MRS. BLANCHARD: No, we didn't know which direction to go in. See, the lifeboats were supposed to be equipped with oars and a compass and food. But ours was just equipped with oars. So, not having any compass we couldn't keep together. And toward morning, why we saw lifeboats scattered all over the place.

JACK GRIMM: One of the lifeboats had two Chinese that were stowaways who were crushed under the seats. Do you have any knowledge of that?

MRS. BLANCHARD. No, I don't know anything about that at all.

JACK GRIMM: Well, thank you very much, Mrs. Blanchard.

MRS. BLANCHARD: You're welcome.

JACK GRIMM: It was a pleasure meeting with you.

MRS. BLANCHARD: It was a pleasure being here, too; thank you very much.

JACK GRIMM: We are sitting in Philadelphia with Miss Eva Hart from England commemorating the seventieth anniversary of the sinking of the *Titanic* this year. She was one of the survivors of the *Titanic*.

EVA HART: It is a great pleasure to be here.

JACK GRIMM: Would you tell us a little about your experiences on the *Titanic*, your age, and some of the memories that you have regarding the sinking of it.

EVA HART: Well, I was seven at the time of the disaster. My memory is absolutely clear and I think one of the reasons is because I was the only child of middle-aged parents who had never in her life heard a disagreement between her parents until we were told that the ship called *Philadelphia*—and it is very strange that I should now be in Philadelphia—the ship on which my father had booked his passage, was not going to sail, because there was a strike. And we were transferred to the *Titanic*. From that moment onward, my mother was smitten, if that is the right word, with a terrible premonition of disaster. And so before we ever went to the *Titanic*, I really was in a terrible state of darkness, because I couldn't understand why my mother was crying as she so often did; I had never seen her cry before. She was saying all the time that she simply couldn't help it. She knew there was something terribly wrong. I didn't know why. And when she saw a headline in the newspaper say that this new ship, the *Titanic*, was unsinkable, she said, "Now I know why I'm frightened. This is flying in the face of God." And that really hit me, as a seven-year-old; you can imagine a child suddenly being told that someone is flying in the face of God. So, long before the *Titanic* sailed, I was very disturbed about this. And that, I think, is one of the reasons that I remember it so clearly.

JACK GRIMM: How many members of your family came to America?

EVA HART: My father drowned. My mother and I were saved. But from the time we went aboard that ship until the dreadful night, my mother never went to bed at night. She sat up all night and slept quite peacefully through the day. And, if my mother had been asleep that night, as I was, and as my father was, and hundreds of other people were, I think there is no doubt that I wouldn't be here talking to you now.

JACK GRIMM: Were you in steerage class?

EVA HART: No, we were in second class.

JACK GRIMM: And were you warned that the ship was in imminent danger of sinking?

EVA HART: The actual time?

JACK GRIMM: Yes; when you first were alerted?

EVA HART: My mother felt this bump. And she used to describe it as a very slight bump, because it was [we were] on the port side of the ship, and as you know, the ship was hit on the starboard side. Because she was wide awake and fully dressed, she wakened my father and me and so we were on deck very early. Had we not been, well, we would have suffered the fate of other people who got on deck too late to get into a lifeboat.

JACK GRIMM: There have been many reports from some of the few survivors from steerage class. They were not warned, and the passageways were locked, and were not opened until the last minute.

EVA HART: That is absolutely true. I look back now and I think there must have been a tremendous number of people aboard the *Titanic* who didn't even know where the boat deck was, because it was divided into three. I can remember playing, as I did with my father on the deck, and suddenly coming across a rope barrier that said, "No Second Class Passengers Beyond This Line." And I have no doubt in the steerage class it said the same thing. I seem to remember the steerage decks were lower than ours, so there must have been a lot of people that didn't know where the boats were.

JACK GRIMM: Did you recall the number of the lifeboat that you and your mother went in?

EVA HART: Well, we started off being put in lifeboat #14, it was hopelessly overcrowded. My father made no attempt to follow my mother and I. He just handed me into my mother and he said, "Now be a good girl and take care of Mummy." And I knew, young as I was, that I would never see him again. It was discovered that this boat that we were in was so overcrowded it couldn't go on. The officer called the boats together and I was just lifted up and taken over the side and put into another boat, while my mother, unbeknownst to me, was taken and put into another boat. What I was eventually in, I don't know. It was impossible to find out, but I do know that it was the last boat to be taken aboard the *Carpathia*.

JACK GRIMM: When the ship sank below the surface, some reports indicate that it may have split in half and a bow or some part of the ship came up to the surface before it sank again. Do you have any recollection of it sinking?

EVA HART: I saw it sink and I was screaming with fright. But my mother, who was a very calm person, despite the fact that she had this premonition, swore to her dying day that the ship was in half.

JACK GRIMM: Yes, we have had many reports to that effect.

EVA HART: She said so. I mustn't say I think it did because I don't know. I think I was too terrified.

MIKE HARRIS: Did you happen to see another ship? Some people talk about seeing a ship close by.

EVA HART: Oh, indeed! Yes! I did. I was screaming why doesn't that ship come?

JACK GRIMM: That has to be the *Californian* then, probably.

EVA HART: You see, all our lives we were told this was the

Californian. Then just a few years back, I don't know whether the story ever reached you here, but it was blazed all over the English newspapers, they said that it was a Norwegian boat that was in the wrong area, and so she just scuttled away before anyone saw her. But I just don't think that could be right. I think that with all the Board of Trade inquiries of all the officers and people who took part in it, I hardly think that they would have said what they did say about the *Californian* if it had not been true.

JACK GRIMM: Well, if it was a Norwegian boat, a fishing vessel, it was in water too deep to be fishing anyway, because you are well off the Grand Banks in 12,000 feet of water; that theory probably doesn't stand up.

I have a photograph that we took on the summer of '81 expedition to look for the *Titanic* of what we believe to be the propeller of it. I am going to show it to you and see if it brings back any recollections or any memories. This is a photograph taken from our television camera sled in 12,500 feet of water. It's transferred to mosaic and put into one piece and you can see the top part of the blade at the top, the curvature. This blade is full face, then it comes down to this point here, and then this blade is at a different angle and then it drops off into the ocean floor but does not touch the ocean floor. This is ocean floor here. So, I believe it is suspended, still attached to the shaft; the ship is here and just out of sight.

EVA HART: It must be; if that is not the ocean floor then it must be attached, mustn't it?

JACK GRIMM: Now, I will show you another. This was a single shot we took of the top part of the blade. Now look at the ocean floor in the background; these clearly are rocks lying on the ocean floor.

EVA HART: Yes.

JACK GRIMM: See how clear the water is?

EVA HART: Yes.

JACK GRIMM: This thing is standing and it's covered with a

leaching effect because salt water is reacting on bronze, and bronze is a combination of copper-tin alloy, but even down in here you can see the bronze color where the pitting has already occurred. So this is the top blade and there is the hub and the bottom blade is down here. This is a blade of a similar ship, the *Oceanic*, that was in the ocean, in the Atlantic, for 62 years. Notice the similarity.

EVA HART: Yes.

JACK GRIMM: And notice the white leaching and pitting effect that both blades have. It was in the ocean some 62 years in the North Atlantic and was salvaged by some Englishmen.

THE FOLLOWING IS A PANEL OF THE SURVIVORS DIS-CUSSING THE DISASTER.

RUTH BLANCHARD: I don't remember how long it was, maybe just a few minutes, but it kept going down, down, down, until the water ran into the boilers and it exploded and made a terrible noise. And the people started jumping from the deck and screaming and that was a very terrible thing to see.

MRS. GOLDSMITH (Widow of Frank Goldsmith): I think Frank told the story at least 2,000 times since 1966, when he first told it to any group at all, which was the Rotarian Club in our hometown in Ohio. And then, he told it to all kinds of groups. He was in collapsible-D, which was the last lifeboat to be lowered at five after two, and they rowed around behind the back of the ship and connected up with the other lifeboats, and then Frank said that his mother covered his eyes so that he couldn't see. Frank was just nine, but she finally let go of his head and he turned and saw this ship straight up in the air, you know, how the pictures show it. And that is the way he remembers it.

EVA HART: I don't know whether that ship broke in half or not, I was so busy screaming myself, when I heard that tremendous explosion. But my mother always declared that that ship went down in two parts. But to me the most horrible moment of all was the sound of people drowning. There could be nothing worse.

GEORGE THOMAS: We were just leaving. We were about half a mile away and at that time we heard screams and people were falling and we looked back and didn't see any more lights at all. The boat had sunk. We just went on until we got to the *Carpathia*, and the *Carpathia* picked us up. I believe our boat was the first one to be picked up. That was lucky for us.

MODERATOR: In some of the recent literature there is some discussion of what went on in the lifeboats after the ship went down, and why the lifeboats didn't go back to pick up some of the people who were in the water, some of them in life jackets, but many of them, of course, not able to last much longer in that cold water. Do any of you recall those discussions in the lifeboats?

GEORGE THOMAS: Our lifeboat went back to pick up more survivors. Then the suction from the *Titanic*—it was going down inch by inch—took the lifeboats that went back. The women got scared and nervous and said we are not going any further. That was the reason we did not go back to pick up more survivors. Had the boats been properly filled in the first place, you could have had a whole boatful of survivors.

RUTH BLANCHARD: We didn't pick up anybody; I don't know how we could have. We were standing up like sardines next to each other. We couldn't possibly have put anybody else in the boat. The men said that one reason they couldn't think of taking anyone in was because they were afraid if we did it would crowd it so that the boat would tip over, and we heard later that there were three that capsized. Mama was sitting by the bed when the *Titanic* hit the iceberg, it shook the boat quite vigorously and then, it hit the iceberg two or three times before it stopped. Then she woke me up and went across the hall to the other cabin. She asked someone to go up on the main deck and find out what was wrong. One of the men went up there and when he came back he told us that the *Titanic* had hit an iceberg and that she had a gash about 300 feet, and to kneel down and pray. Well, Mother said, "I will pray, but I think I am going to see if I can save my life and my children's life," and then she came into our cabin and took me up out of it. Mama took my hand and took me up on the main deck. Then she told me to wait there till she could go back to one of the cabins. and we ended up next to the lifeboats; that's when we left the *Titanic*.

BIBLIOGRAPHY

Baptist, Captain, C.N.T. *Salvage Operations*. London: Stanford
    Maritime, Limited, 1979.

Beesley, Lawrence. *The Loss of the S.S. Titanic*. Boston: Hough-
    ton Mifflin Company, 1912.

Bullock, Shan F. *A Titanic Hero: Thomas Andrews Shipbuilder*.
    Riverside, Ct. 7 C's Press, [1912] 1973.

Conrad, Joseph. "Some Aspects of the Admirable Inquiry." *The
    English Review*, II, (1912), pp. 581–95.

Culliton, Barbara J. "Woods Hole Mulls Titanic Expedition."
    Science, 197, (August 26, 1977), pp. 848–49.

Gracie Archibald. *The Truth About the Titanic*. New York: M.
    Kennerley, 1913.

Grossett, Harry. *Down to the Ships in the Sea*. Philadelphia: J.B.
    Lippincott Co., 1954.

Hoffer, William. *Saved!: The Story of the Andrea Doria—The
    Greatest Sea Rescue in History*. New York: Summit Books,
    1979.

Lightoller, Charles H. *Titanic and Other Ships*. London: Ivor Nicholson and Watson, 1935.

Lord, Walter. *A Night to Remember*. New York: Holt, Rinehart & Winston, 1955.

Marcus, Geoffrey. *The Maiden Voyage*. New York: The Viking Press, 1969.

Miller, Byron S. *Sail, Steam and Splendour*. New York: Times Books, 1977.

Muckelroy, Keith. *Maritime Archaeology*. Cambridge, Cambridge University Press, 1978.

Padfield, Peter. *The Titanic and the Californian*. New York: The John Day Company, 1965.

Stackpole, Edouard A. *Those in Peril on the Sea*. New York: The Dial Press, 1962.

Throckmorton, Peter. *Shipwrecks and Archaeology: The Unharvested Sea*. Boston: Little, Brown & Company, 1970.

————. *Diving for Treasure*. New York: The Viking Press, 1977.

Wade, Wyn Craig. *The Titanic: End of a Dream*. New York: Rawson, Wade Publishers, Inc., 1979.

Walker, John. *An Unsinkable Titanic*. New York: Dodd, Mead & Company, 1912.

Winocour, Jack, ed., *The Story of the Titanic as Told by Its Survivors*. New York: Dover Publications, Inc., 1960.

INDEX